THE ADLARD COLES NAUTICAL QUIZ BOOK

ADLARD COLES NAUTICAL

BLOOMSBURY

LONDON • NEW DELHI • NEW YORK • SYDNEY

Published by
Adlard Coles Nautical
an imprint of Bloomsbury Publishing Plc
50 Bedford Square, London WC1B 3DP
www.adlardcoles.com

First published by Adlard Coles Nautical in 2014

ISBN 978-1-4729-0913-8
ePDF 978-1-4729-1638-9
ePub 978-1-4729-1637-2

A CIP catalogue record for this book is available from the British Library.
This book is produced using paper that is made from wood grown in managed, sustainable forests. It is natural, renewable and recyclable. The logging and manufacturing processes conform to the environmental regulations of the country of origin.

Typeset in Frutiger and Sabon
Printed and bound in Great Britain by CPI Group (UK) Ltd, Croydon CR0 4YY

10 9 8 7 6 5 4 3 2 1

Created and produced for Adlard Coles Nautical by Ivy Contract
SENIOR EDITOR: Judith Chamberlain-Webber
DESIGN: Kelvin Hughes
Quizzes compiled by Jane Moseley, Jackie Strachan and Malcolm Garrard

Introduction

This book is for savvy seafarers and sailors in search of some serious fun. In the cockpit, cabin or car, round the kitchen table, on a boat, train, ferry or plane, on the way to far-flung islands or fogbound off your local coast: wherever you are, the carefully crafted 1,000 questions (you don't need to count!), divided both thematically and then by degree of difficulty, will keep you entertained for hours, if not days. There are so many fascinating facts to test each other on and to learn. Even the most know-it-all friend or member of the family will be foxed by some of them. Dip into one of the six categories: geography, history, culture, famous people, science and trivia. Each category is divided into three grades: easy 'able seaman', medium 'midshipman' or tough 'hard tack'. Mix and match to customise your own quiz, picking a round from each category, or stick to a chosen subject. Make it as easy or hard as you like. It's that simple. A sprinkling of nautical 'did-you-knows' adds a little salt to the mix and there's a quick-fire section at the end to keep everyone on their toes.

It's all about the what, when, where, who, how, why and 'wow, I didn't know that!' There is something for everyone – those just getting their sea legs and salty old sea dogs.

The *Nautical Quiz Book* should float everybody's boat.

Grade: Able Seaman

1. In which large northerly country is the magnetic North Pole located?

2. From which city did John Cabot set out on his Atlantic voyages: (a) Bristol, England (b) Lisbon, Portugal (c) Cartagena, Spain?

3. Which ocean is approximately 106 million square km (41 million square miles) in size: (a) Arctic (b) Indian (c) Atlantic?

4. Which wind blows from the Sahara Desert across the Mediterranean Sea?

5. What two bodies of water does the Canal du Midi in France link?

6. Where is the United States Naval Academy situated: (a) Annapolis, Maryland (b) Chicago, Illinois (c) Miami, Florida?

7. Near which Scandinavian country would you find the Moskstraumen?

8. In which African country does the Cape Doctor blow?

9. Which is the largest Caribbean island: (a) Martinique (b) Cuba (c) Saint Lucia?

10. What is the world's busiest port by cargo tonnage: (a) New York (b) Rotterdam (c) Shanghai?

Grade: Able Seaman

11. What is an anemometer?

12. Which country has the shortest coastline in Europe?

13. What is the northern terminus of the Suez Canal?

14. Which islands near Argentina are part of the UK?

15. What was the name of the first permanent English settlement in the New World?

16. Where is the Strait of Magellan?

17. What are the Roaring Forties?

18. In which ocean is the Bermuda Triangle?

19. Where does the Round the Island race start from?

20. In which country is the island of Java?

Grade: Able Seaman

21. On which coast of North America is the novel *The Shipping News* set?

22. In which sea are the Lesser Antilles islands?

23. Which waterway joins the Atlantic and Pacific oceans?

24. Which wind can often cause fierce storms in the Mediterranean between Corsica and the Balearics?

25. Where would you find the temperate zones?

26. To what geographical feature did the explorer Henry Hudson give his name?

27. Where did the *Exxon Valdez* run aground and spill her oil in 1989?

28. Name the five principal oceans of the world.

29. What is the name of the powerful, warm Atlantic current that originates at the Gulf of Mexico?

30. Which European port city was hit by an earthquake and tsunami in 1755?

Did you know?

Whales are the largest animals on earth, swallowing up to half a million calories in a single mouthful.

Grade: Able Seaman

31. In which archipelago would you find the island of La Palma?

32. Which wind force is equivalent to 6.5–11km/h (4–7mph)?

33. Which of these islands belongs to Denmark:
(a) Sicily (b) Greenland (c) Iceland?

34. What great feat of engineering was opened to ships in 1869?

35. What island is named after a winter festival?

36. What is the deepest natural harbour in the world:
(a) Sydney Harbour (b) Portsmouth Harbour (c) New York Harbour?

37. What is the warmest sea in the world:
(a) The Baltic Sea (b) The Red Sea (c) The North Sea?

38. Name one of the two records the Dead Sea holds.

39. What are the Needles?

40. Where is the Cape of Good Hope?

Grade: Able Seaman

41. What is the smallest sea in the world: (a) The Red Sea (b) The Black Sea (c) The Sea of Marmara?

42. Which country has the longest coastline in the world: (a) Norway (b) Canada (c) Russia?

43. What is the main port in the Gulf of Lion in the south of France?

44. Which city is famous for its canals?

45. From which language does the word 'tsunami' come?

46. How many main islands are there in the Ionian archipelago: (a) Seven (b) Ten (c) Fifteen?

47. Where would you find the littoral zone of a body of water?

48. Across the bay of which West Coast US city does the Diablo wind blow?

49. What do the letters ITCZ stand for?

50. What is a tidal bore?

Grade: Able Seaman

51. In which ocean was the *Mary Celeste* discovered?

52. Which Portuguese port is twinned with Bordeaux in France and Bristol in the UK?

53. Which island in New York is home to the Statue of Liberty?

54. Which two countries are separated by the Bering Strait?

55. Which sea is the setting for 21 of Shakespeare's 38 plays?

56. List the five Great Lakes (in order of size if you can!)

57. What is the difference between an ocean and a sea?

58. Which way do fluids flow in the Northern Hemisphere?

59. In which Russian city is the Neva Bridge raised to let tall ships pass?

60. What is El Niño and where would you find it?

Did you know?

The word for breeze comes from the Spanish *briza*, meaning a light wind.

Grade: Midshipman

61. Where is the deepest part of the Pacific Ocean?

62. Calshot Castle protects the mouth of which UK stretch of water: (a) The Thames Estuary (b) The Serpentine (c) Southampton Water?

63. Where did the Greek Pytheas of Massalia visit around 325 BCE: (a) Modern-day Syria (b) Persia (c) The British Isles and the Atlantic coast of Europe?

64. Which port on the Adriatic has the largest annual turnover of cargo: (a) Split, Croatia (b) Port of Trieste, Italy (c) Dubrovnik, Croatia?

65. Where would you expect to encounter the Furious Fifties?

66. If you were looking down from Devil's Peak, what port would you see?

67. Why did Ferdinand Magellan name the ocean he entered the 'Mar Pacifico'?

68. What body of water in the Southern Ocean is named after a Scottish navigator: (a) MacDougall's Straits (b) Patrick's Channel (c) The Weddell Sea?

69. Which island in the Far East was known as Formosa to early sailors: (a) Taiwan (b) Christmas Island (c) Seram Island?

70. From which port did RMS *Titanic* sail and at which ports did she call en route?

Grade: Midshipman

71. Which small peninsula was ceded to Britain 'in perpetuity' by the Treaty of Utrecht in 1713?

72. Which Belgian town used to be a port linked by canals to the sea?

73. Which sea route connects the Atlantic and Pacific oceans through the Arctic Ocean?

74. What is the Nore:
(a) A preserved lighthouse in Connecticut (b) A sandbank at the mouth of the Thames Estuary (c) A rock around which a race is sailed from the Royal Cork Yacht Club every 2 September?

75. Which body of water is bounded by China, Taiwan, the Philippines, Malaysia, Brunei, Indonesia, Singapore and Vietnam?

76. Which river flows into the headwaters of Chesapeake Bay in the USA?

77. Which Atlantic island was claimed by Portugal in 1420?

78. Where does Santiago battle with a marlin in Hemingway's *The Old Man And The Sea*?

79. What is the name of the southernmost tip of South Africa: (a) Cape Point (b) Cape of Good Hope (c) Cape Agulhas?

80. What type of canal is the Panama Canal?

Grade: Midshipman

81. Where does the squamish wind blow: (a) Along the narrow fjords of British Columbia, Canada (b) Through the Strait of Gibraltar (c) North to south down Chesapeake Bay?

82. Name the world's three longest rivers in order of length.

83. In which Scandinavian city would you find Djurgårdsbrunnskanalen?

84. A tour around the harbour of which European city would take in the Speicherstadt?

85. In which British city would you find the 'floating harbour' and what is it?

86. How many million square kilometres does the Pacific Ocean cover: (a) 155 (b) 255 (c) 364?

87. Which South African port is nicknamed 'The Friendly City': (a) Cape Town (b) Durban (c) Port Elizabeth?

88. Where would you find the Trade Winds?

89. How big was the tallest ocean wave ever recorded: (a) 9m (30ft) (b) 23m (75ft) (c) 27m (90ft)?

90. Which is the only sea defined by ocean currents rather than land boundaries?

Grade: Midshipman

91. What is the strong easterly wind in the Mediterranean, especially in the Strait of Gibraltar, called?

92. Where is the greatest tidal range on Earth: (a) Bay of Fundy, Canada (b) Port of Bristol, England (c) Gulf of St. Malo, France?

93. What is a Mulberry Harbour?

94. Which nation began exploring the Atlantic coast in the early 15th century under the sponsorship of Prince Henry the Navigator?

95. Of which nation are the ABC Islands in the Caribbean Sea a part?

96. Where does the violent, squally wind known as the Tehuantepecer originate?

97. What was the original name for the Cape of Good Hope?

98. Where is Drake Passage?

99. Name the notorious wind of the western Mediterranean that blows across parts of the Mediterranean Sea.

100. Where can you sail under the longest bridge in Europe?

Grade: Midshipman

101. Which Atlantic islands were claimed by Portugal in 1427?

102. Which is the largest passenger port on the Adriatic Sea?

103. Which body of water is the hottest:
(a) Bay of Bengal (b) Persian Gulf (c) Caribbean Sea?

104. Which is the highest navigable lake in the world?

105. What is distinctive about the Caspian Sea?

106. Which is the busiest port on the East Coast of the USA:
(a) Baltimore (b) Miami (c) The Port of New York and New Jersey?

107. Where are the headquarters of the Russian Navy:
(a) Gorky Park, Moscow (b) Admiralty Building, St Petersburg
(c) Navy Prospekt, Odessa?

108. Which landlocked nation did Shakespeare unexpectedly endow with a sea coast in *A Winter's Tale*:
(a) Bohemia (b) Austria (c) Bolivia?

109. Where is the Pacific Tsunami Warning System based?

110. Where does the UK Meteorological Office have its headquarters:
(a) London (b) Oxford (c) Exeter?

Grade: Midshipman

111. What was recorded at Lituya Bay, Alaska, at a height of 524m (1,719ft)?

112. Where were the sailing events held for the 2012 Summer Olympics?

113. In which country is the Tanner Cup contested: (a) Wales (b) New Zealand (c) South Africa?

114. What is a Bora?

115. What is the largest island in the Mediterranean Sea: (a) Corfu (b) Majorca (c) Sicily?

116. 'Sail south until the butter melts.' To what does this advice relate?

117. What is the Acqua Alta?

118. Which sea conditions are associated with Force 5 on the Beaufort Scale?

119. Approximately how many islands, islets, reefs and cays are there in the Caribbean Sea: (a) At least 700 (b) More than 7,000 (c) No one knows for sure?

120. How many bridges cross Chesapeake Bay in the USA?

Did you know?

Throwing a ship's cat overboard was thought likely to bring on a storm.

Grade: Hard tack

121. What warning flags are flown to alert of hurricane force winds?

122. Which island is recognised as being the site of John Cabot's landfall on 24 June 1497?

123. How many islands make up Tonga: (a) 36 (b) 170 (c) 302?

124. What was the 'Protestant wind'?

125. Name at least one of the destinations of the three long-distance voyages completed by HMS *Beagle*.

126. Where do the warm Mozambique-Agulhas current from the Indian Ocean and the cool Benguela current from Antarctic waters converge?

127. What is the deepest lake in the world?

128. Which capital city was the venue for the sailing events at the 1980 Moscow Olympics?

129. Which port in New Zealand is also known as Poneke?

130. Where in South-east Asia would your boat be taken by the Kuroshio current?

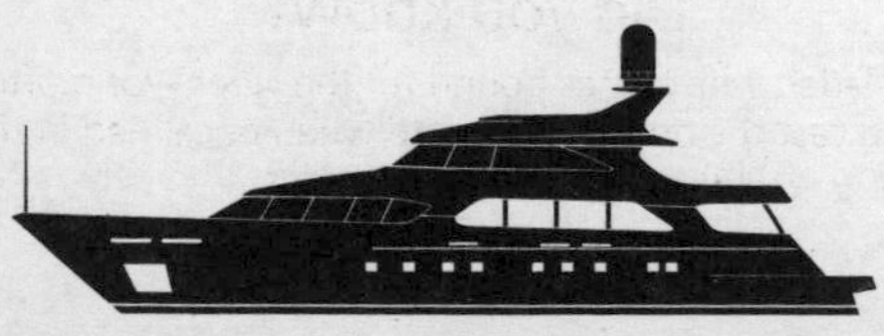

Grade: Hard tack

131. When was the first Russian circumnavigation of the Earth?

132. In which Caribbean archipelago is Blackbeard's Castle?

133. How many major islands make up the Hawaiian Islands: (a) Six (b) Eight (c) Fifteen?

134. Where does the Marin wind blow?

135. Which two bodies of water are connected by the Lombok Strait?

136. Name three of the six countries the Mekong River flows through.

137. What is the capital of the US Virgin Islands?

138. What is an atoll?

139. Where is the world's largest mobile harbour crane to be found: (a) Belfast (b) The Port of Vancouver (c) Toronto?

140. Where did Erskine Childers sail in *The Riddle of the Sands*?

Did you know?

Ships laden with horses bound for the New World often had to cast the horses overboard when becalmed in the so-called 'horse latitudes'.

Grade: Hard tack

141. On your round-the-world trip, which five southern capes will you have to round?

142. Which port on the African mainland is still a Spanish exclave?

143. What was the name for the celestial navigation device first used by Arab navigators to find latitude: a) A kamal (b) A sextant (c) An astrolabe?

144. What is the longest river in Europe?

145. Which current is responsible for carrying icebergs into the North Atlantic shipping lanes?

146. Where did Christopher Columbus's crew first sight land when they reached the Americas?

147. Where does the Coromuel wind blow?

148. Name the smallest shallow sea covering the continental shelf of Europe.

149. What is the Western name for the body of water known as Nan Hai?

150. Where is the windiest place in the world: (a) Wellington, New Zealand (b) Chicago, USA (c) Commonwealth Bay, Antarctica?

Grade: Hard tack

151. How are tornadoes measured?

152. Which US city is known as Waterfront Wonderland, with over 640km (400 miles) of waterways?

153. Which UK pier was renamed HMS Leigh during World War II?

154. In which country is the compass thought to have been invented: (a) Spain (b) Egypt (c) China?

155. Where did William Willis single-handedly sail on his raft *Seven Little Sisters* in 1954?

156. What is the American Mediterranean Sea?

157. Where in South-east Asia would you find the Macclesfield Bank?

158. What are the SSS islands?

159. Where did the most devastating tsunami in modern times strike in 2004?

160. Where is the Vineyard Race held?

Did you know?

'Mare's tales and mackerel scales make tall ships take in their sails' is an old weather saying about clouds.

Grade: Able Seaman

1. What nationality was Christopher Columbus?

2. Vasco da Gama opened up trade to which continent in 1498?

3. What was Sir Walter Raleigh's post:
(a) Captain (b) Commander (c) Naval advisor?

4. In which country was Ferdinand Magellan born?

5. Which famous admiral was born in Norfolk, UK?

6. Which US president and his wife were famous for their love of yachting?

7. By what name is Edward Teach better known?

8. Name one of the first two Europeans to circumnavigate the world.

9. What record did Dame Ellen MacArthur set in 2001?

10. Who set sail on HMS *Beagle* on 27 December 1831?

Grade: Able Seaman

11. Which UK prime minister in the 1970s had a boat called *Morning Cloud*?

12. What was Sir Walter Raleigh incorrectly credited with doing?

13. Which famous captain and explorer was born in 1728 in the Yorkshire village of Marton in England?

14. Who was the first sailor to circumnavigate the globe non-stop westwards in 1971?

15. Who was Bartholomew Roberts?

16. Who was Jackie Kennedy's famous shipping father?

17. What European nationality was Henry the Navigator?

18. Which island did Abel Tasman find in 1642 that was later named after him in his honour?

19. What was Vice Admiral William Bligh most famous for?

20. William Hillary founded a British institution for boat rescue in 1824; what was it?

Did you know?

Sir Ernest Shackleton recorded in his Antarctic diaries that his horses suffered badly in the stormy weather, probably from seasickness.

Grade: Able Seaman

21. How many adults joined Noah on his Ark: (a) Four (b) Seven (c) Nine?

22. Who or what was Davy Jones's locker?

23. What signal did Admiral Lord Nelson send to the fleet on the morning of the Battle of Trafalgar?

24. Who discovered a strait at the tip of South America in 1520 and gave his name to it?

25. Who was the captain of RMS *Titanic* when it sank?

26. Which UK actor who starred in *The Mission* has raced in the BT Global Challenge?

27. Who was the first explorer to cross the Antarctic Circle: (a) Ferdinand Magellan (b) Sir Francis Drake (c) Captain James Cook?

28. What piece of nautical equipment did the English clockmaker John Harrison invent?

29. How many days did Frenchman François Gabart take to complete and win the 2013 Vendée Globe, setting a new record: (a) Just over 78 (b) Nearly 81 (c) Over 100?

30. Whose boat was the *Gypsy Moth IV*?

Grade: Able Seaman

31. Which cat served on Sir Ernest Shackleton's *Endurance*: (a) Mrs Chippy (b) Mrs Ratty (c) Ginger?

32. Which famous US pirate's treasure remains undiscovered?

33. Who led the mutiny on HMS *Bounty*?

34. Which privateer, whose name is associated with an alcoholic drink, became governor of Jamaica?

35. What is named after Francis Beaufort?

36. Which famous English admiral became Baron of the Nile in 1798?

37. Which fictional character was Captain Flint?

38. Which racing championship yachtsman founded his own British publishing company in 1947?

39. Which famous US Postmaster General was the first person to describe and chart the Gulf Stream?

40. Who was the first woman to perform a single-handed circumnavigation via Cape Horn: (a) Dame Naomi James (b) Dame Ellen MacArthur (c) Dame Mary Peters?

Grade: Able Seaman

41. Which part of his body did Admiral Lord Nelson lose in Tenerife?

42. Which famous ship did Vice-Admiral Robert Fitzroy command in 1828?

43. Which brutal Roman Emperor built two huge ships at Lake Nemi in the 1st century CE: (a) Nero (b) Julius Caesar (c) Caligula?

44. Which yachtsman holds the record for the most gold medals at successive Olympics?

45. Which famous female sailor sailed the *Kingfisher*?

46. On what ship did Sir Ernest Shackleton set off to cross the Antarctic from the Weddell Sea to the Ross Sea in 1914?

47. What did Dutch sailor Laura Dekker achieve in 2012?

48. Which UK explorer disappeared trying to navigate a section of the Northwest Passage in 1847: (a) Rear Admiral John Franklin (b) Rear Admiral Clarence Brown (c) Rear Admiral James Wallace?

49. Name at least one of the pair of sailors who rowed across the Atlantic Ocean in 1966 in *English Rose III*?

50. Who were the two female crew members who sailed with pirate Calico Jack?

Grade: Able Seaman

51. What should merchant sailors thank Samuel Plimsoll for?

52. Which Danish sailor has won four gold Olympic medals and world championships in eight different classes?

53. Which Beatle took a 965km (600 mile) voyage from Rhode Island to Bermuda in 1980 to clear his writer's block?

54. Name one of the two possible figures the warship *Mary Rose* is named after.

55. Who sailed round the world at the age of 65 in 1966/7?

56. Which famous actor who starred in *Casablanca* gave his name to a race from Newport to Catalina Island?

57. Which US teenager set out on an epic solo voyage in 1965 on a 24ft (7m) sailing boat?

58. Where and when was Admiral Lord Nelson killed?

59. Which gold medal-winning British sailor drowned after capsizing in San Francisco Bay in 2013?

60. How many nautical miles was Robin Knox-Johnston's voyage round the world: (a) 25,325 (b) 27,503 (c) 30,123?

Did you know?

The ship's mascot on RMS *Titanic* was a cat called Jenny.

Grade: Midshipman

61. What event is lighthouse-keeper William Darling and his daughter Grace famous for?

62. What did Harry Pidgeon achieve in the early 20th century:
(a) First person to solo circumnavigate the globe
(b) First person to solo circumnavigate the globe twice
(c) First person to circumnavigate the globe east to west?

63. What book did the pioneering meteorologist Robert Fitzroy publish in 1863?

64. What ship did Christopher Jones take across the Atlantic in 1620?

65. Why did Sir Francis Drake leave Plymouth twice in 1577?

66. Which World War II statesman was photographed patting Blackie, the ship's cat on the HMS *Prince of Wales*?

67. Which US female sailor competed aboard *America* in the 1992 America's Cup?

68. Which Japanese admiral commanded the attack on Pearl Harbor in December 1941?

69. What type of vessel did Cornelius Drebbel build in 1620:
(a) The first navigable submarine (b) The first navigable catamaran
c) The first functioning dredger?

70. Who died aboard the *Quest* on January 1922 in South Georgia?

Grade: Midshipman

71. Which British monarch was nicknamed the 'Sailor King': (a) King Henry VIII (b) Charles II (c) King William IV?

72. What was the name of the head designer of the RMS *Titanic* who went down with the vessel?

73. Who was the captain of the *Mary Celeste* when she was discovered unmanned and drifting in 1872?

74. On which schooner did Roald Amundsen leave Oslo for the South Pole in 1910?

75. What sailing first did Ann Davidson achieve in 1952?

76. Which European probably reached the New World 500 years before Christopher Columbus?

77. Which French yachtsman smashed Dame Ellen MacArthur's solo round-the-world record in 2008 by more than 14 days?

78. Which famous entrepreneur owns the *Necker Belle* yacht?

79. Which yachtsman led Team New Zealand to victory in the America's Cup in 2000?

80. What did Teddy Seymour achieve:
(a) The first African-American to sail solo around the world (b) The first blind yachtsman to sail solo around the world (c) The first man to sail solo across the Atlantic without navigational instruments?

Grade: Midshipman

81. What was pirate Calico Jack's real name: (a) John Rackham (b) Jack Johnson (c) John Ransom?

82. What name meaning 'dragon' did the Spanish give Sir Francis Drake?

83. What did Norwegian Thor Heyerdahl build from papyrus?

84. Who completed the first single-handed circumnavigation in recorded history, completed in 1898?

85. Which two dukes led the Spanish fleet in the Spanish Armada?

86. Name the woman who survived the sinking of RMS *Titanic* and the HMS *Britannic* four years later: (a) Eloise Smith (b) Violet Jessop (c) Ethel Beane.

87. Who was the skipper of the British boat *Hugo Boss* that finished third in the 2013 Vendée Globe?

88. Who was named Commander-in-Chief of the Royal Navy's Mediterranean Fleet in June 1939?

89. Which James Bond actor served as an anti-aircraft gunner in the Royal Navy?

90. Who skippered the first all female crew in the Whitbread Round the World Race?

Grade: Midshipman

91. What did Paul Larsen achieve on *Vestas Sailrocket 2* in 2012?

92. Who commanded the SS *United States* on her maiden voyage: (a) Commodore Harry Manning (b) Commodore Leroy Alexanderson (c) Commodore John Anderson?

93. São Gabriel, São Rafael and São Miguel were all in the armada of which Portuguese explorer?

94. Who became Commander-in-Chief of the Pacific Ocean Areas in 1942: (a) Chester W Nimitz (b) Robert L Ghormley (c) William Halsey Jr?

95. What was the name of the steel yacht David Lewis sailed around the Antarctic alone in 1972?

96. Which English diarist became Chief Secretary to the Admiralty under King Charles II and King James II?

97. Which son of a famous potter funded Charles Darwin's voyage on HMS *Beagle*?

98. Which British grandmother sailed solo around the world non-stop in 2013?

99. Which 19th-century US captain noted for his courage is said to have shouted in the middle of battle: 'I have not yet begun to fight.'?

100. What did Dee Caffari achieve in 2006?

Grade: Midshipman

101. Doris Miller was the first African-American to be awarded the Navy Cross during which World War II attack?

102. Which ocean were Norwegians Frank Samuelson and George Harbo the first to row across in 1896?

103. Who achieved the first ever single-handed vertical navigation of the globe in 2008: (a) Adrian Flanagan (b) Sir Robin Knox-Johnston (c) Dame Ellen MacArthur?

104. What first did Myrtle 'Molly' Kool, born in 1916, become?

105. Which ships did the Pinzon brothers captain on Christopher Columbus's expedition?

106. Which US president said 'Control of the seas can mean peace. Control of the seas can mean victory.': (a) President John F Kennedy (b) President George Bush Jr (c) President Richard Nixon?

107. Name the raft Thor Heyerdahl used to cross the Pacific Ocean.

108. In which powerboat did Richard Branson break the record for crossing the Atlantic in 1986?

109. Which famous mutineer is possibly the inspiration for Samuel Taylor Coleridge's poem 'The Rime of the Ancient Mariner'?

110. Where did Ferdinand Magellan lose his life: (a) In the Philippines (b) In the Caribbean (c) In the Atlantic Ocean?

Grade: Midshipman

111. Which explorer was the first to sail the Northwest Passage?

112. What medal did Hannah Mills and Saskia Clark of Britain win in the 470 Women's Class at the 2012 London Olympics?

113. Admiral Hugh Palliser said this about which English sea captain: 'The ablest and most renowned navigator that this or any country hath produced'?

114. Which great Romantic poet met his death in 1822 in a boat called *Don Juan*?

115. Who became the fastest Briton to sail around the world in a monohull boat in 2013?

116. Which African-American actor sailed for the first time in 1967 and has been hooked ever since?

117. Who was known as the 'Grace Darling of America'?

118. Which English admiral lost his life in a shipwreck off the Isles of Scilly in 1707: (a) Admiral Sir Cloudesley Shovell (b) Admiral Sir John Cloudesley (c) Admiral Sir Cloudesley Lovell?

119. Which British sailor was awarded the Chevalier de la Légion d'Honneur in 2008?

120. Which female Australian sailor unofficially became the youngest person to sail non-stop unassisted around the world in 2010?

Grade: Hard tack

121. Name Sir Ben Ainslie's great Danish rival in the 2012 Olympics.

122. What was the nickname of Admiral Andrew Browne Cunningham (1883–1963)?

123. Who was the first skipper in the world to cross the 50-knot sailing speed barrier aboard *Hydroptere*: (a) Alain Thébault (b) Éric Tabarly (c) Alain Delord?

124. Who became Commander in Chief of the United States Fleet in 1941?

125. How did Jeanne Baret disguise herself when she sailed around the world in the 18th century: (a) A man (b) A pirate (c) A stowaway?

126. Which French sailor abandoned winning the Golden Globe Race in 1969 and sailed on to the South Pacific?

127. Who was in charge of Sir Walter Raleigh's abortive sea venture in 1587: (a) John White (b) Philip Amadas (c) Arthur Barlowe?

128. What was remarkable about William Brown, who joined the Royal Navy in 1804?

129. Who served as First Lord Commissioner of the Admiralty for most of the Seven Years' War in Europe (1756–1763)?

130. In 1998, who was the first African-American woman to hold the rank of Rear Admiral in the US Navy?

Grade: Hard tack

131. Which US sailor born in 1942 was known as 'Mr America's Cup'?

132. Admiral William Brown (1777–1857) was known as the 'Father' of which navy: (a) The Argentine (b) The British (c) The American?

133. Navigator William Adams is thought to have been the first Englishman to reach which country in 1600: (a) Japan (b) China (c) Australia?

134. How was Giovanni Caboto better known?

135. What animal nickname did Napoleon give to Admiral Lord Thomas Cochrane?

136. What was US Navy Lieutenant Matthew Fontaine Maury (1806–73) famous for: (a) Oceanography (b) Navigation (c) Metereology?

137. Which sailor saved fellow competitor Alex Thomson in the Velux 5 Oceans yacht race in 2006?

138. With which famous adventurer's sword was Sir Francis Chichester knighted by Queen Elizabeth II in 1967?

139. What was the name of the captain who was the last to leave the RFA *Sir Galahad* during the Falklands War in 1982: (a) Captain Philip Roberts (b) Captain Linley Middleton (c) Captain Jeremy Black?

140. Who tried to make a permanent settlement on Roanoke Island, America, in an abortive sea venture in 1587?

Grade: Hard tack

141. Who became a national hero on Christmas Day in 1996 after rescuing a fellow competitor in the Vendée Globe race?

142. How did American naval officer Samuel Francis du Pont end his career in the American Civil War?

143. Which famous ship was commanded by Commodore W E Warwick in 1969 and later by his son in 1990?

144. Why were Samson, Shakespeare and Surley on board *Endurance*?

145. Who was the most successful pirate of the Golden Age of Piracy, taking over 470 prizes in his career?

146. Which German leader commissioned the building of the vessel known as the *Ostwind*?

147. Which yachtsman, awarded the Chevalier de la Légion d'Honneur, drowned in the Irish Sea in 1998?

148. Which island in the Pacific Ocean did Dutch explorer Jacob Roggeveen encounter on a notable Sunday?

149. Captain Eduard Brickenstein was captain of which ill-fated iron passenger steamship in 1875:
(a) SS *Deutschland* (b) SS *Muenchen* (c) SS *Dusseldorf*

150. Who was the first American to sail in three America's Cups and two Whitbread Round the World races?

Grade: Hard tack

151. Which Frenchman holds the record for sailing around the Isle of Wight: (a) Michel Desjoyeaux (b) Éric Tabarly (c) Vincent Riou?

152. Which Italian explorer had observed the Hudson River 85 years before Henry Hudson?

153. Name the first female sailor to row solo across three oceans: the Pacific, Atlantic and Indian.

154. Who was the first North American woman to row solo across the Atlantic from Canada to France in 2013?

155. Which English peer sailed across the Atlantic single-handedly and wrote the book *Where the Ocean Meets the Sky*?

156. The navigation skills of Captain Harry Manning of USS *United States* assisted which famous female aviator?

157. Which sailor single-handedly circumnavigated the Southern Ocean through the Roaring Forties during World War II?

158. Where did Welsh pirate Bartholomew Roberts finally meet his fate?

159. Who skippered a crew of paratroopers, that took line honours in the Whitbread Round the World Race in 1973?

160. Winston Churchill worked closely with which First Sea Lord in fighting the German battleship threat in 1939–40?

Grade: Able Seaman

1. Which northern European nation used the knorr for long sea voyages?

2. On large sailing ships, what was the aftcastle: (a) An elevated structure at the bow (b) An elevated structure at the stern?

3. Name one of the three ancient civilisations that used the galley as a warship.

4. What is the oldest type of boat ever found, dating back about 8,000 years to the Neolithic Stone Age?

5. What was a broadside in terms of a warship: (a) The side of a ship (b) A cannon battery (c) The firing of all the cannon on one side of a ship simultaneously?

6. Which oil tanker was shipwrecked off England's Cornish coast in 1967 causing an environmental disaster?

7. In which year did Ferdinand Magellan set sail on the expedition that would lead to the first circumnavigation of the globe: (a) 1495 (b) 1519 (c) 1620?

8. What kind of trousers did sailors traditionally wear?

9. Where was the Tudor warship *Mary Rose* discovered?

10. Which ex-prison hospital ship achieved glory at the Battle of Trafalgar in 1805?

Grade: Able Seaman

11. How many tiers of oars were there in a trireme?

12. In steamships, what did the screw propeller replace in the early 19th century?

13. How was a galley powered in ancient times?

14. Which iron-hulled steamer built by Isambard Kingdom Brunel was the first to cross the Atlantic?

15. Why did the RMS *Lusitania* sink off the coast of Ireland in 1915?

16. What was built on Eddystone Rocks, Plymouth, England in 1698?

17. What was the original grog?

18. Which disease did European ships take to England in 1347?

19. In medieval ships, men armed with what type of weapon would often be stationed on the forecastle?

20. What is the USS *Constitution*'s nickname and where can she be seen?

Did you know?

Ching Shih (aka Cheng I Sao) was a female Chinese pirate who commanded over 1,500 ships.

Grade: Able Seaman

21. What cargo did the clipper *Cutty Sark* transport: (a) Sugar (b) Tea (c) Oranges?

22. Which city did the Spanish Armada sail from in 1588: (a) Cadiz, Spain (b) Cartagena, Spain (c) Lisbon, Portugal?

23. How was meat traditionally preserved on board ship?

24. What was a powder monkey?

25. What was the Impress Service more commonly known as?

26. What was a 'lighter', found on rivers up until the 1960s?

27. What weapon was a naval ram?

28. How was Lord Admiral Nelson's body brought home after the Battle of Trafalgar?

29. What was the name of the boat used by Greenpeace as an environmental campaign ship?

30. What was the punishment for piracy in 19th-century Britain?

Grade: Able Seaman

31. What kind of vessel was an ironclad?

32. Which shipping line owned the RMS *Titanic*?

33. What class of ship was the USS *Yorktown*: (a) A passenger ship (b) An aircraft carrier (c) A destroyer?

34. In addition to five support and supply vessels, there were six other ships in the fleet that left Britain for Australia in 1787 – what did they transport?

35. What was a hen frigate: (a) A ship used to transport livestock b) A ship with the captain's wife on board (c) A small ship?

36. On what river did the first recorded yacht race take place in 1661: (a) The Amazon (b) The Hudson (c) The Thames?

37. What was hardtack?

38. What use were some large decommissioned ships put to in the late 18th–19th centuries: (a) Floating prisons b) Hospital ships (c) For training sailors?

39. How were thieves traditionally punished in the British Navy: (a) Flogged in front of the crew (b) Made to run the gauntlet of the crew armed with knotted ropes (c) Beaten on the soles of the feet with sticks?

40. What type of boat was built by shipyards on the US mid-Atlantic coast: (a) Yarmouth yawl b) Baltimore clipper (c) Boston schooner?

Grade: Able Seaman

41. What was the advantage of the original 'line of battle' tactic?

42. How many of the original 237 men on Ferdinand Magellan's first circumnavigation of the earth returned: (a) 18 (b) 67 (c) 105?

43. What was the purpose of RMS *Titanic*'s fourth funnel?

44. What were the first crow's nests made of?

45. What was the name given to the small group of men with whom a sailor would eat: (a) Talley (b) Mess (c) Barney?

46. What did the oarsmen in Viking longships sit on: (a) The bare deck (b) Sea chests containing their personal possessions (c) Their shields?

47. What is the oldest trophy in international sport?

48. Which Roman emperor commissioned two 'Nemi barges' in the 1st century CE: (a) Caligula (b) Tiberius (c) Claudius?

49. Which peoples are thought to have developed the lateen sail: (a) The Arabs (b) The Greeks (c) The Egyptians?

50. The wreck of which ship is a popular dive site in the Great Barrier Reef Marine Park, Australia: (a) *Mermaid* (b) *Centaur* (c) *Yongala*?

Grade: Able Seaman

51. What was a man o'war?

52. Name the first ship to reach the site of RMS *Titanic*'s sinking.

53. How were the first narrowboats powered?

54. In what war were submarines first used widely?

55. How many voyages did Christopher Columbus make to the New World: (a) One (b) Four (c) Eight?

56. What fuel was burned in Argand lamps, used in early lighthouses?

57. Which British battleship launched in 1906 gave its name to a class of battleships?

58. What nationality was the ARA *General Belgrano*, sunk in 1982?

59. How many sails did a Viking longship have?

60. What was Greek fire: (a) Combustible material used to set fire to enemy ships b) A fiery sunset over the Mediterranean Sea c) An ineffective cannon broadside?

Did you know?

Hoskyn was the ship's cat on HMS *Chester* during the Battle of Jutland in 1916, alongside the captain's sheepdog.

Grade: Midshipman

61. What speed is the trireme thought to have been able to achieve in short bursts in calm conditions: (a) 8 knots (15km/h) (b) 12 knots (22 km/h) (c) 15 knots (28 km/h)?

62. In which battle did Fleet Admiral William 'Bull' Halsey oversee the Allied naval forces in 1944: (a) Battle of Leyte Gulf b) Battle of Midway (c) Battle of Solent Point?

63. Which nation built the first ocean-going ironclad battleship *Gloire*?

64. Which group of people did the *Susan (Sarah) Constant*, the *Discovery* and the *Godspeed* transport?

65. Name the shipping line that owned RMS *Mauretania*.

66. The RMS *Titanic* sank approximately 640km (400 miles) off the coast of which large Canadian island?

67. English navigator Captain Matthew Flinders was the first man to circumnavigate which continent in the early 19th century?

68. How many rowers was the tessarakonteres said to have had: (a) 40 (b) 400 or (c) 4,000?

69. Approximately how many calories a day did a seaman consume in Horatio Nelson's navy: (a) Around 1,000 (b) Around 2,500 (c) Around 5,000?

70. What were Liberty Ships and when were they used?

Grade: Midshipman

71. Which fore-and-aft sail succeeded the square sail?

72. What was the largest naval engagement of World War I, fought between the British, Australian and Canadian navies and the German fleet?

73. Where did Elizabeth I make her famous speech to the troops on 19 August 1588, allegedly before her battle with the Spanish Armada?

74. How many miles did Christopher Columbus's ships average in a day: (a) 80km (50 miles) (b) 160km (100 miles) (c) 193km (120 miles)?

75. In the Napoleonic era, what rank was a midshipman in the Royal Navy?

76. What type of boat was a 'buss': (a) A fishing boat for catching herring (b) An early form of passenger ferry (c) An aboriginal canoe?

77. What type of hull construction was common in the Mediterranean during the Middle Ages: (a) Clinker (b) Flat bottom (c) Carvel?

78. Whose fleets did Octavian defeat at the Battle of Actium in 31 BCE: (a) Antony and Cleopatra's (b) Ptolemy and Cleopatra's (c) Caesar and Cleopatra's?

79. What is the name of the tool used to plane hull surfaces as far back as Egyptian times?

80. In which year did the only vessel to return safely from Sir Francis Drake's round-the-world expedition arrive in Plymouth Sound: (a) 1510 (b) 1540 (c) 1580?

Grade: Midshipman

81. What was the name of the only five-masted, full-rigged ship ever built, with no auxiliary engine: (a) *Preussen* (b) *Saltzen* (c) *Wanderhaven*?

82. Where did Brunel plan for the steamship SS *Great Eastern* to sail to from the UK without refuelling?

83. In the 18th and 19th centuries, what was a frigate?

84. The tarred corpse of which pirate hung at Tilbury Point on the Thames in England for several years: (a) Edward Teach (b) William Kidd (c) Henry Morgan?

85. Which nation developed the carrack in the 15th century: (a) Spain (b) Ireland (c) Portugal?

86. What kind of sail did the clinker-built cog have?

87. In the ancient world, what was the difference between the way warships and merchant ships were powered?

88. Name the oldest surviving commissioned warship in the world, launched in 1765.

89. The *Charles W. Morgan* is the only surviving ship of her kind, in Connecticut, USA; what was her trade?

90. In what year was the New York Yacht Club founded: (a) 1844 (b) 1884 (c) 1904?

Grade: Midshipman

91. What was the orlop deck?

92. What was a Higgins boat?

93. What kind of vessel was the *Turtle*, built in 1775 in Connecticut, USA?

94. Which bark was used to cover Native American canoes: (a) Oak (b) Birch (c) Maple?

95. How many times in five minutes could a broadside be fired by an efficient gun crew in the late 18th century: (a) Two or three (b) Four (c) Five?

96. What happened to the Swedish warship *Vasa* on her maiden voyage in 1628?

97. How did the original cruisers get their name?

98. What unusual material was the Irish currach traditionally made of?

99. Where and how can you see the wreck of the USS *Arizona*?

100. Who were the Jack Tars?

Did you know?

In a severe storm, Christopher Columbus is said to have placed his report to the Queen of Castile into a cask and thrown it into the sea.

Grade: Midshipman

101. What was unusual about the shape of the Russian warship *Novgorod*, launched in 1873?

102. With which insurance company is the ringing of the Lutine Bell associated?

103. What surprise tactic did the English fleet deploy to great effect when faced with the Spanish Armada?

104. In which country can you see the ancient Khufu ship?

105. Which World War II German battleship was named after a famous Prussian chancellor?

106. Where were the cancelled 1940 Olympic sailing races due to be held?

107. What did the sailors do on the Russian battleship *Potemkin* in 1905?

108. What was the daily ration of small (weak) beer in the English fleet at the time of the Spanish Armada:
(a) 2 pints (1.1 litres) (b) 4 pints (2.2 litres) (c) 1 gallon (4.5 litres)?

109. Where did the Barbary pirates come from:
(a) North Africa (b) The Caribbean (c) Spain?

110. Which German admiral gave his name to a Bismarck-class battleship?

Grade: Midshipman

111. Which nation sank Greenpeace's *Rainbow Warrior* in 1985?

112. Off which coast in the southern hemisphere is the wreck of the *Loch Ard*?

113. Name one of the areas you would find on the lowest deck of a warship.

114. Which English king took part in the first recorded yacht race in 1661?

115. What mobile navigation and warning device was first installed at the mouth of the Thames in England in 1732?

116. What happened to the large Danish ship *Kobenhavn* in 1928: (a) She sank (b) Her captain jumped overboard (c) She mysteriously disappeared without trace?

117. Which year was the Royal Australian Navy created: (a) 1788 (b) 1803 (c) 1859?

118. What was unusual about the naval Battle of Midway fought between the Japanese and US fleets?

119. Which is said to be the oldest yacht club in the world, founded in 1720?

120. Which country established the first European colony on the Virgin Islands: (a) The Netherlands (b) England (c) France?

Grade: Hard tack

121. Which Mediterranean island was being fought over in the Battle of Lepanto in 1571?

122. Which nation developed the caravel in the 15th century: (a) The Spanish (b) The Dutch (c) The Portuguese?

123. Name the first submarine to sink an enemy vessel.

124. Five British ships have borne the name *Ark Royal*. What famous naval engagement did the first take part in?

125. Which fleet did the Persians fight at the Battle of Salamis in 480 BCE?

126. What class of vessel is the USS *Thresher*, wrecked east of Boston, Massachusetts, USA, in 1963?

127. Around which Scottish islands was the wooden boat called a birlinn used: (a) The Hebrides (b) The Shetlands (c) The Orkneys?

128. Name the German ocean liner that took the Blue Riband from RMS *Mauretania* in 1929: (a) SS *Frankfurt* (b) SS *Rinteln* (c) SS *Bremen*?

129. What weapons did the submarine USS *Robert E Lee* carry?

130. What was the Dutch jacht used for hunting: (a) Whales (b) Pirates (c) Cod?

Grade: Hard tack

131. The *Mary Rose* was sunk in 1545. What year was she raised: (a) 1971 (b) 1982 (c) 1988?

132. What was significant about the ships in the Battle of Hampton Roads in the American Civil War?

133. The sinking of which ship caused the largest non-military loss of life: (a) RMS *Titanic* (b) MV *Doña Paz* (c) RMS *Lusitania*?

134. What was a penteconter?

135. Put the founding of these nautical races in chronological order: America's Cup, Sydney Hobart, Fastnet.

136. What is the name of the lens invented in 1821 and installed in many lighthouses?

137. Name one of the two ancient powers which fought the Battle of Ecnomus off Sicily in 256 BCE?

138. In the Ancient Roman navy, what was the corvus: (a) A walkway dropped onto an enemy ship to board it (b) The crow's nest (c) A battering ram?

139. Approximately when was the cloth sail first developed: (a) 3300 BCE (b) 200 BCE (c) 50 CE?

140. What was notable about the ships that fought the Battle of Lepanto in 1571?

Grade: Hard tack

141. In which decade was the first *Queen Mary* liner built: (a) 1920s (b) 1930s (c) 1950s?

142. What was the Korean 'turtle ship' and why was she unusual?

143. Which group of people rebelled on the *Amistad* in Cuba in 1839?

144. From which part of the world did Western sailors first pick up the practice of tattooing: (a) Indonesia (b) The Caribbean (c) Tahiti and the Polynesian islands?

145. What was the original name and nationality of the United States Lines flagship SS *Leviathan*?

146. Name the ship commanded in 1588 by Sir Francis Drake in the battle against the Spanish Armada: (a) HMS *Revenge* (b) HMS *Elizabeth* (c) HMS *Victory*?

147. Mutiny and murder took place among the survivors of which ship wrecked off the coast of Australia in 1629: (a) *Moravia* (b) *Sumperk* (c) *Batavia*?

148. What was notable about the design of the liner the RMS *Empress* of France?

149. What is the Tower of Hercules and where can you find it?

150. Name the Italian explorer-navigator from whose name the term 'Americas' is derived.

Grade: Hard tack

151. What kind of vessel was the *Sea Witch*, launched in 1846: (a) A clipper (b) A cargo ship (c) A passenger ship?

152. Name one of the three German cruisers nicknamed 'pocket battleship'.

153. Which notorious English pirate was second-in-command to Benjamin Hornigold at the start of his career?

154. Name the first vessel to reach the North Pole in 1958.

155. How many times did the submarine HL *Hunley* sink, causing a danger to her crew: (a) Once (b) Three (c) Five?

156. To which boat and where was the first America's Cup awarded?

157. In what war did the naval battles of Plymouth and Port Royal take place?

158. What was a gam: (a) A type of spar (b) A punishment (c) A social meeting of the crews on board whaleships at sea?

159. Which famous explorer's crew mutinied in Canadian waters on the *Discovery* in 1611?

160. Which sea route did the Portuguese mariner Gil Eanes open up in 1434?

Grade: Able Seaman

1. Which swashbuckling Australian actor stars in the 1940 film *The Sea Hawk*?

2. Which of the characters in Kenneth Grahame's *The Wind in the Willows* spends most of his time on the river?

3. Name the author of the epic poem which contains this quotation: 'Lord Odysseus was happy as he set his sails to catch the breeze.'

4. What is the name of the big musical number sung by the sailors in the musical *South Pacific*?

5. Who went to sea 'in a beautiful pea-green boat' and what did they take with them?

6. What event is depicted in Théodore Géricault's painting *Raft of the Medusa*?

7. By what two names is the god of the sea known in Greek and Roman mythology?

8. In which Disney film does the sea witch Ursula appear?

9. Who wrote *Ice Station Zebra* featuring the nuclear submarine USS *Tigerfish*?

10. What is the next line in John Masefield's poem 'Sea Fever': 'I must go down to the seas again, to the lonely sea and the sky'?

Grade: Able Seaman

11. Which Jamaican musician wrote and sang 'Many Rivers to Cross'?

12. In which archipelago is Staffa, the island that inspired Felix Mendelssohn's *Fingal's Cave*?

13. What kind of straw hat is the man in Édouard Manet's *Boating* wearing?

14. What does the god Neptune (aka Poseidon) carry?

15. What does the crew of the US submarine find at the bottom of the oceanic trench in the film *The Abyss*?

16. What was *Proud Mary* in the eponymous song by Creedence Clearwater Revival: (a) A river boat (b) A lighthouse (c) A canoe?

17. Which English composer wrote the opera *Billy Budd*?

18. Who sang about the Bermuda Triangle in 1981?

19. Name the opera written by Gilbert & Sullivan featuring a ship.

20. What is the *Pirates of the Caribbean* film series based on?

Grade: Able Seaman

21. Which French verb is the term 'shanty' derived from?

22. What are the Swallows and Amazons in the book of the same name?

23. Which rock band recorded 'The Seven Seas of Rhye'?

24. Which Impressionist painted *The Grand Canal Venice*?

25. In the film *Finding Nemo*, what is clownfish Dory's problem?

26. Which 20th-century US author wrote *The Old Man and the Sea*?

27. Sing the next line in this sea shanty: 'Come all ye young fellows that follow the sea'.

28. Which real-life father and daughter star in the 1981 film set on a lake, *On Golden Pond*?

29. What creature is described as follows? 'There she blows! – there she blows! A hump like a snow-hill!'

30. Who immortalised HMS *Temeraire* on canvas?

Did you know?

John Steinbeck's first novel *Cup of Gold* is based on the life of privateer Henry Morgan.

Grade: Able Seaman

31. What happens to the ship in the 1972 film *The Poseidon Adventure*?

32. The design of which famous opera house resembles a series of upturned shells or sails?

33. Which famous rock band member did Johnny Depp base his *Pirates of the Caribbean* character Captain Jack Sparrow on?

34. Which rock band sang about a message in a bottle?

35. Who are the baddies in The Beatles' animated film *Yellow Submarine*?

36. Which children's classic novel are these quotes from: 'That was Flint's treasure that we had come so far to seek' and 'Yo-ho-ho and a bottle of rum!'?

37. What kind of a boat is *The African Queen* in the novel and film of the same name?

38. In which musical does a boat cross an underground lake beneath an opera house?

39. Which Russian emperor is the ship sculpture on the Moskva River in Moscow dedicated to?

40. What is the nationality of the pirates who take Captain Phillips hostage in the 2013 film of the same name?

Grade: Able Seaman

41. Who had a big hit with 'Sailing' in 1975?

42. Who wrote 'The Rime of the Ancient Mariner' and what creature does the Mariner shoot?

43. What is the name of the brigantine in the children's classic book *Peter Pan* and what does it refer to?

44. In Greek mythology, what was the name of the Argonauts' ship and who was their leader?

45. How many times has the story of the mutiny on *The Bounty* been filmed: (a) Twice (b) Three times (c) Five times?

46. Where do the adventures of fictional character Huckleberry Finn take place?

47. Handel's suite of orchestral pieces *Water Music* was premiered on a barge on which English river: (a) The Thames (b) The Severn (c) The Tyne?

48. Most of the land is underwater in the film *Waterworld*. What event has caused the flooding?

49. What is the name of the ship that Captain Ahab commands in *Moby-Dick*?

50. In which ocean does the shipwreck in Yann Martell's *Life of Pi* take place?

Grade: Able Seaman

51. What was the name of the song performed in the 1997 film *Titanic* and who sang it?

52. What famous piece of needlework portrays the Norman fleet invading England?

53. Which British singer-songwriter had a hit with 'Sail Away' in 2001?

54. Who said: 'Believe me, my young friend, there is nothing – absolutely nothing – half so much worth doing as simply messing about in boats.'?

55. The legendary sea monster the kraken is usually portrayed as what?

56. Which pop group made the Bahamian folksong 'The John B. Sails' into a huge hit?

57. What is the name of the dance most commonly associated with sailors?

58. Which Italian artist, whose name means 'little canal', is well known for his waterscapes?

59. On which vessel is the film *The Crimson Tide* set: (a) Spanish galleon (b) US nuclear submarine (c) Norwegian cruise ship?

60. Who had a hit with 'Orinoco Flow (Sail Away)'?

Grade: Midshipman

61. What is Long John Silver's parrot called and what does it say?

62. Which film is based on the true event of an ill-fated school sailing trip in 1961: (a) *White Squall* (b) *The Sheltering Sky* (c) *Into the Blue*?

63. Which 19th-century US poet, better known for his poem about an Indian hero, wrote these lines: 'Till my soul is full of longing, For the secret of the sea'?

64. Which vessel sailed from Nantucket in 1819 and features in Nathaniel Philbrick's novel *In the Heart of the Sea*?

65. In what hymn do the verses end with the refrain: 'For those in peril on the sea'?

66. Which colours complete the title of the work by James Abbott McNeill Whistler: *Symphony in… and… : The Ocean*: (a) *Blue and Green* (b) *Blue and Grey* (c) *Grey and Green*?

67. Which South American river is the Yacumama sea monster said to live in?

68. Who or what is the wolf in Jack London's novel *The Sea-Wolf*?

69. Which French composer wrote the movement 'En Bateau (Sailing)'?

70. Which US writer and Transcendentalist said this about the sea: 'If you can hold me, I am the key to all the lands.'?

Grade: Midshipman

71. Which 1970s' pop trio wrote the song 'Southern Cross' about a man who sails around the world following a failed love affair?

72. Which French port does Claude Monet's *Impression, Sunrise* depict: (a) Harfleur (b) Le Havre (c) Calais?

73. Name either of the two leading characters in the series of novels by Patrick O'Brian that begins with *Master and Commander*.

74. In which film does Errol Flynn cut a sail with his knife so he can slide down it onto the deck:
(a) *The Sea Hawk* (b) *Captain Courageous* (c) *Captain Blood*?

75. In the sea shanty 'South Australia', name the woman that the sailors meet.

76. Which 20th-century Welsh poet wrote: 'Though I sang in my chains like the sea'?

77. Name the composer of the song cycle *Sea Pictures*:
(a) Sir Edward Elgar (b) Felix Mendelssohn (c) Benjamin Britten?

78. Which port did the *Irish Rover* sail from in 1806 and where was she bound for, in the song of the same name?

79. In the 2004 film *The Life Aquatic*, what creature does Bill Murray's character set out to take revenge upon?

80. Who wrote the series of novels featuring Horatio Hornblower?

Grade: Midshipman

81. Where on a ship was the shanty 'Homeward Bound' usually sung?

82. Identify the Polish-born author of this quote, and the novel it comes from: 'There is nothing more enticing, disenchanting, and enslaving than the life at sea.'

83. Which real-life castaway is said to have inspired Daniel Defoe's novel *Robinson Crusoe*?

84. Where was Winslow Homer's painting *A Fair Wind* (or *Breezing up*) reproduced in small scale?

85. What kind of vessel features in the book and film *The Cruel Sea* and what is its role?

86. Which famous cartoon character appears in the animated film *Steamboat Willie*: (a) Donald Duck (b) Mickey Mouse (c) Popeye?

87. Which explorer does the Singing Ship Monument in Emu Park, Queensland, Australia, commemorate?

88. 'On a trim Black Ball liner I first served my time' is from *Blow the Man Down*. What was the Black Ball Line?

89. Name the first line and title of the poem and song that continues: 'A-home on the rolling deep!'

90. Which river is featured in the song 'Ol' Man River' from the musical *Show Boat*?

Grade: Midshipman

91. Apart from Mount Fuji, what was the 19th-century Japanese artist Katsushika Hokusai most famous for painting?

92. In the musical *On the Town,* in which town are the three US sailors taking shore leave:
(a) New York (b) Philadelphia (c) Boston?

93. In *The Talented Mr Ripley*, what happens when Dickie and Ripley take a boat out together?

94. What rips a hole in the boat of the character played by Robert Redford in the 2013 film *All is Lost*:
(a) A shark (b) A storm (c) A rogue container?

95. Who co-wrote and performed the song 'Blue Bayou'?

96. What African river features in Joseph Conrad's *Heart of Darkness*:
(a) The Zambezi (b) The Congo (c) The Limpopo?

97. Name one of the three stars in the 1989 film of Charles Williams' novel *Dead Calm*.

98. In Norman Rockwell's illustration *Tattoo Artist*, what is the tattooist doing to the sailor's arm?

99. By what name is Samuel Langhorne Clemens better known?

100. What is the name of the 2000 film about a boat that sank in a cyclone off the Massachusetts coast?

Grade: Midshipman

101. Which 17th-century Dutch artist painted *The Storm on the Sea of Galilee*?

102. Which English composer wrote the one-act opera *Riders to the Sea*?

103. In Walt Whitman's 'O Captain! My Captain!', what relationship is the 'Captain' to the narrator?

104. Name the captain and his vessel from Jules Verne's *Twenty Thousand Leagues under the Sea*.

105. Name the pirate played by Geoffrey Rush in the *Pirates of the Caribbean* film series.

106. Where is the monument to Henry the Navigator situated: (a) Lisbon (b) Cadiz (c) Genoa?

107. Name at least one of the leading roles in Wagner's *The Flying Dutchman*.

108. Which superhero actor made his 1978 film debut in *Gray Lady Down*?

109. Which US writer had a beloved fishing boat, *Pilar*, named after his wife Pauline?

110. In Greek mythology what kind of water creature is the Hydra?

Grade: Midshipman

111. What does the title of the film *Das Boot* mean?

112. What is the mythical Lorelei said to do?

113. Who wrote the novel *Jaws*?

114. What is the name of the third novel in the Aubrey-Maturin series by Patrick O'Brian: (a) *Post Captain* (b) *Desolation Island* (c) *HMS Surprise*?

115. Name the US realist painter of *Max Schmitt in a Single Scull* and *Starting Out After Rail*: (a) Edward Hopper (b) Edward Leigh Chase (c) Thomas Eakins?

116. Name the French composer of the exuberant concert overture evoking a seascape, *Le Corsaire*.

117. In Greek mythology, who carried the souls of the departed across the River Styx?

118. What is the title of artist Ivan Aivazovsky's best-known work depicting shipwreck survivors clinging to a lone mast in a heavy sea?

119. Name one of the two stars of the 1959 film comedy about a pink submarine, *Operation Petticoat*.

120. Name the ship on which Long John Silver sets sail in *Treasure Island*, named after a tropical island.

Grade: Hard tack

121. Who wrote the popular song 'La Mer': (a) Serge Gainsbourg (b) Charles Trenet (c) Jacques Brel?

122. Which award-winning fantasy novel charts the exploits of puppeteer John 'Jack Shandy' Chandagnac?

123. In what orchestral suite does the movement 'The Sea and Sinbad's Ship' feature and who is the Russian composer?

124. Which 19th-century US artist is best known for paintings such as *The Fog Warning*?

125. What quality does the Russian submarine *Red October* possess?

126. Who is the skipper describing in this poem by Henry Wadsworth Longfellow: 'And he saw her hair, like the brown seaweed, On the billows fall and rise'?

127. What is the name of the single from rock band Pearl Jam's debut album *Ten* that relates to the sea?

128. Which Lebanese writer said: 'In one drop of water are found all the secrets of all the oceans.'?

129. Name the British marine painter of *HMS* 'Britannia' *Entering Portsmouth* and *A Sailing Boat in a Fresh Breeze off Cowes*.

130. Where are the miniaturised submarine and crew of sci-fi film *Fantastic Voyage* sent on their mission?

Grade: Hard tack

131. Which English singer-songwriter wrote and recorded the haunting 'River Man'?

132. Which 19th-century US mystery writer is the author of the short story 'MS. Found in a Bottle'?

133. What is Frederic's problem in *The Pirates of Penzance*?

134. What was displayed temporarily on the fourth plinth in London's Trafalgar Square in 2012?

135. In Celtic folklore, what kind of creature is a kelpie and what could it transform itself into?

136. What wreck did Gordon Lightfoot sing about?

137. Who wrote about his sloop the *Spray*, and what was the title of his memoir?

138. In which Asian city can you see a vast statue of Admiral Yi Sun-Sin: (a) Tokyo (b) Kuala Lumpur (c) Seoul?

139. In the 2000 film *U-571*, the German U-boat is boarded by US submariners. What espionage device are they looking for?

140. Which Shakespearian character sings a song that begins as follows, and in which play:
'Full fathom five thy father lies;
Of his bones are coral made'?

Grade: Hard tack

141. What do the Cape Cod girls use to brush their hair in the shanty of the same name?

142. From which 1840 memoir does this quote come, as the boat rounds Cape Horn: 'At the end of each watch when we came below, we took off our clothes… Stockings, mittens, and all were… hung up to drain.'?

143. Name Lieutenant Pinkerton's ship in *Madame Butterfly*.

144. Where can you see the ship sculpture *Sun Voyager* by Jón Gunnar Árnason: a) Stockholm b) Oslo c) Reykjavik?

145. Which English actor is described as the 'patron saint' of Talk Like a Pirate Day?

146. Which sea shanty bidding goodbye to a Canadian province does this refrain come from: 'For when I am far away on the briny ocean tossed, Will you ever heave a sigh or a wish for me?'

147. Which Irish-American playwright spent several years at sea and wrote *Seven Plays of the Sea*?

148. Who is the author of *Bluewater Sailor*, the third book in a trilogy about life aboard a US Navy destroyer.

149. Name the Scottish poem that features the witch Cutty-sark.

150. Which famous 19th-century sea battle does Sir Henry Wood's *Fantasia on British Sea Songs* commemorate?

Grade: Hard tack

151. How many ships are depicted in *The Stages of Life* by Caspar David Friedrich (a) Five (b) Seven (c) Nine?

152. In the 1982 film *Fitzcarraldo*, is a riverboat: (a) Hauled over a hill (b) Towed along a canal by horse (c) Hauled through village streets?

153. Which ship appears in Henry Wadsworth Longfellow's poem 'Paul Revere's Ride'?

154. Name the clipper in which Sherlock Holmes and Watson chase the villain in *The Sign of Four*: (a) *Aurora* (b) *Morgana* (c) *Merlin*.

155. Which comic actor stars in the 1928 film *Steamboat Bill Jr*?

156. Which ship (named after an American frontiersman) features in the song 'The Leaving of Liverpool'?

157. 'It really is the most ridiculous and useless machine that the spirit of man could conceive.' What type of sailing boat is Samuel Pepys describing?

158. Upon which vessel does Count Dracula sail to Whitby?

159. In 2012, who wrote *Blue Water, Green Skipper: A Memoir of Sailing Alone Across the Atlantic*, about his experiences of crossing the ocean single-handedly?

160. In which sea shanty is the first line of the chorus: 'We will rant and we'll roar like true British sailors'?

Grade: Able Seaman

1. How many tides are there usually in a day?

2. What is another name for a sea anchor: (a) Log (b) Pogue (c) Drogue?

3. What is a sextant used for?

4. What is the function of a wind scoop?

5. Where does a gyroscopic compass tend to point?

6. What is latitude?

7. What is longitude?

8. What city is to be found at coordinates 51°30′26″N, 0°7′39″W: (a) London (b) Montreal (c) Bilbao?

9. What is a main halyard used for?

10. Which astronomical feature has been named after an explorer: (a) Cook Galaxy (b) Magellanic Clouds (c) Cabot Cluster?

Grade: Able Seaman

11. What does CQR stand for:
(a) Come quickly, rescue (b) Nothing, the CQR originally was going to be called the 'secure' anchor (c) Cum quod ratio?

12. What is a tide table?

13. What causes waves at sea?

14. Why is a sextant called a sextant?

15. What is a beam reach?

16. What is a thwart?

17. What is a becket: (a) The pole on which a sextant was balanced (b) A removable guardrail at the transom (c) A short length of rope, sometimes with the ends joined?

18. What is the purpose of the crow's nest?

19. How could you indicate a vessel is in distress using only flags?

20. What is a rhumb line?

Did you know?

Over the yardarm means about 11 o'clock in the morning (when the sun appears over the ship's yardarm in the North Atlantic).

Grade: Able Seaman

21. Where is the clew of a sail?

22. What were the very first personal flotation devices made of?

23. What does it mean to scandalise a sail: (a) To tell it the 'it's your turn in the barrel' joke (b) To reduce sail (c) To use an old sail as patching material?

24. Why are the waters at Cape Horn so notoriously tricky?

25. What is hull speed?

26. What does SOS stand for?

27. Which undersea means of communication was called the Eighth Wonder of the World?

28. What were 19th-century lifejackets made of: (a) Balsa wood (b) Lead (c) Cork?

29. What is a turk's head?

30. What is a tsunami?

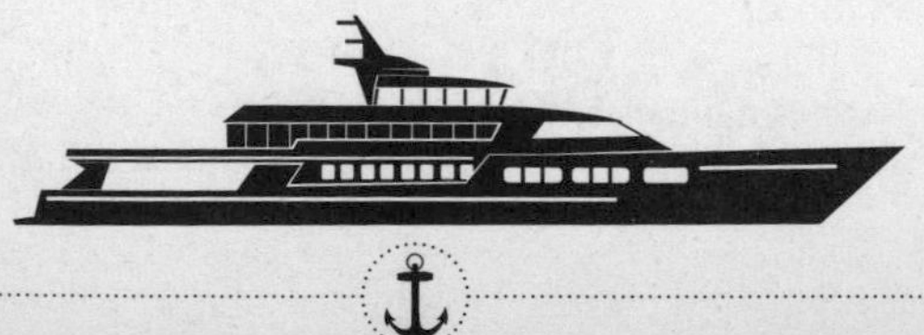

Grade: Able Seaman

31. Where would you find a fluke and what is its purpose?

32. Approximately, what percentage of seawater is actually dissolved salts: (a) 3.5 per cent (b) 5 per cent (c) 50 per cent?

33. What marks on a buoy indicate safe water: (a) Horizontal stripes (b) Vertical stripes (c) A zigzag pattern?

34. What was scattershot?

35. What is wind shear?

36. Which part of the body is the first to be affected by seasickness: (a) The stomach (b) The brain (c) The heart?

37. What is significant about the hulls of most modern oil tankers: (a) They are painted with anti-climb paint (b) They have a double hull (c) They slope in towards the deck above the waterline?

38. What is slack water?

39. Why are objects more buoyant in salt water than fresh water?

40. What marks or lights must an anchored sailboat display?

Did you know?

Changing the name of a ship is thought to bring bad luck.

Grade: Able Seaman

41. Which is denser, cold or warm water?

42. What is a dry dock?

43. What was the 'black goose' that had to be skinned, not plucked, encountered by Magellan in South America?

44. What large air-cushion vehicle is used at sea?

45. Which islands were the scene of Darwin's observations of mockingbirds and tortoises?

46. Which port is to be found at coordinates 33°51′35.9″S 151°12′40″E: (a) Manila (b) Beijing (c) Sydney?

47. Which famous vessel lies at an approximate depth of 3.8km (2.4 miles/12,500ft)?

48. What is a bowsprit?

49. What does it mean to be 'in irons'?

50. What is a mizzen mast?

Did you know?

One seaman's proverb goes: 'The ship that will not obey the helm will have to obey the rocks.'

Grade: Able Seaman

51. What is bareboating: (a) Self-hire yacht chartering (b) Sailing naked (c) Operating a boat with no electronic assistance?

52. Where might you find a pulpit on board a boat?

53. What is a gybe?

54. Where would you look for a transom on a boat?

55. What is scrimshaw:
(a) Decoration of ivory or bone objects (b) Dividing up the possessions of a dead comrade (c) Slacking off work?

56. What is a bascule bridge: (a) A bridge with no superstructure (b) An opening bridge (c) A bridge with a central support?

57. Why were early boats tarred?

58. What is running:
(a) Motor sailing without using the mainsail
(b) Sailing a boat with the wind about 30° either side of dead downwind (c) Sailing with all sails fully deployed?

59. What is the term for the tendency of a vessel to come up into wind when sailing close hauled and heavy on the helm: (a) Griping (b) Sniping (c) Wiping?

60. What is the international calling and distress channel?

Grade: Midshipman

61. Name two of the three aerodynamic forces that act upon a sailboat under way.

62. The extra curve of material added to a triangular sail to provide more power and lift is known as a: (a) Roach (b) Coach (c) Loach?

63. What is the name given to the glowing condition of the sea sometimes seen at night?

64. What was grapeshot?

65. What is special about the Mercator projection?

66. What is the difference between a wave and a swell?

67. What is the rule of twelfths?

68. Which star is sometimes called the seaman's star and why?

69. What is hydrodynamics?

70. What was a holystone used for: (a) Finding true north (b) Onboard wedding ceremonies (c) Scrubbing wooden decks?

Did you know?

Nautical astronomer Tycho Brahe's tame elk is said to have died by drinking too much beer and falling down the stairs.

Grade: Midshipman

71. What is a moonraker:
(a) A small light sail on a square rigged ship (b) A device for cleaning an ironclad's hull (c) A boathook with a double hook?

72. What is the difference between a nautical mile and a knot?

73. What 1930s female film star's name was given to a type of jib used on board a few large racing boats:
(a) Louise Brooks (b) Greta Garbo (c) Barbara Stanwyck?

74. Where would you be unlucky enough to find a supercell?

75. A piece of low-lying ice, broken away from ice packs or icebergs and difficult to see from a vessel because of its dark colour, is known as a: (a) Growler (b) Prowler (c) Sowler?

76. Unexplained lights at sea are known as:
(a) Nelson's lantern (b) Davy Jones' balefire (c) Teach's lights?

77. What type of weapon was a carronade?

78. Who used a sun shadow board:
(a) The Romans, to measure distances (b) The Phoenicians, to measure time (c) The Vikings, to check bearings?

79. Who used a nocturnal and why?

80. What do lateral buoys indicate: (a) Dangerous wrecks (b) The borders of channels (c) The extent of a no-sail zone?

Grade: Midshipman

81. Who first used copper to sheathe a hull and when: (a) The British Royal Navy in the 18th century (b) The Greeks in the 3rd century BCE (c) Dutch merchants in the 16th century?

82. What is the Saffir-Simpson scale?

83. What was a Mae West in terms of safety gear?

84. What does an isobar indicate?

85. At what approximate distance from the planet's surface do GPS satellites orbit the Earth: (a) 40,400km (25,100 miles) (b) 20,200km (12,600 miles) (c) 10,100km (6,300 miles)?

86. When entering a channel in Europe, Australasia and Africa, on which side are the red marks and lights?

87. What is an EPIRB?

88. What lights are required of a powered vessel underway?

89. What is a meteotsunami?

90. What call (including the word 'mayday') means that the channel should be used only by the vessel in distress and the coastguard?

Grade: Midshipman

91. What is hydrography?

92. If you pass buoy number 4 followed by number 5 in a channel, are you heading into port or out to sea?

93. Where is the safe water around a west cardinal buoy: (a) To the west (b) To the east (c) Both west and east, as it indicates current?

94. What happens when a plough-in occurs on a hovercraft?

95. What is the purpose of a sea anchor?

96. What term was coined by Ivan T Sanderson in 1962 to describe an unidentified organic mass washed up on the seashore: (a) Globster (b) Flobster (c) Blobster?

97. What is the benthic zone: (a) A temperate zone just north and south of the Equator (b) The lowest level of a body of water (c) The area immediately in front of the bow of a yacht?

98. When entering a channel in the Americas, Japan, Korea and the Philippines, on which side are the red marks and lights?

99. At what distance would you expect to be able to see a light in dense fog (code no. 0): (a) More than 100m (330ft) (b) 75m (246ft) (c) Less than 50m (164ft)?

100. How many satellites are needed to give an accurate GPS position: (a) Two (b) Three (c) At least four?

Grade: Midshipman

101. Name two of the main symptoms of scurvy.

102. What percentage of the Earth's surface is covered by water: (a) 65 per cent (b) 71 per cent (c) 78 per cent?

103. What lights are required of a sailing vessel underway?

104. Where is the international dateline?

105. What is a maelstrom?

106. How many fuel tanks does the average oil tanker have: (a) Between 8 and 12 (b) Between 50 and 100 (c) Up to 500?

107. A device to stop or limit the boom's ability to swing across the centreline of the boat unexpectedly, for example during a gybe, is known as a: (a) Gripper (b) Preventer (c) Intruder?

108. What is the international distress message in voice radio communications?

109. What is a Bermuda rig?

110. Why might you require a leech line?

Grade: Midshipman

111. Why are battens added to a sail?

112. A flat-bottomed boat with a blunt bow is known as a: (a) Ketch (b) Yawl (c) Scow?

113. What is freeboard?

114. What is an outhaul used for in a Bermuda-rigged boat?

115. What is the difference between a jib and a genoa?

116. What is the name of the physical effect that enables a boat to sail as fast as or faster than the wind: (a) Bernoulli's principle (b) Gillan's law (c) Dynamic tension?

117. What is the name given to the electrical discharge which under certain atmospheric conditions can take place at mast heads or yardarms of a ship: (a) St Mark's embers (b) St Elmo's fire (c) St Ian's combustion?

118. What is the marine VHF frequency range?

119. What is 'bobbing a light'?

120. What is a boat's camber?

Grade: Hard tack

121. What is barratry:
(a) A legal term for the intentional damage of a vessel or its cargo
(b) The legal term for what was commonly known as 'press-ganging'
(c) The legal term for running a gambling den for seamen?

122. William Froude established experiments to show the stability of ships in a seaway. Was he born in: (a) 1710 (b) 1810 (c) 1910?

123. What geographical process of interest to sailors was described in Aristotle's *Meteorology* in 350 BCE: (a) The hydrological cycle (b) The hydroponic cycle (c) The hydrometeorological cycle?

124. What is raking fire?

125. When was the first weather map published in *The Times*: (a) 1875 (b) 1895 (c) 1920?

126. In nautical astronomy, what is the zenith?

127. What is forked mooring?

128. What is a seiche: (a) A large lake fed by more than one river (b) A standing wave oscillating in a body of water (c) A small tsunami?

129. What is the greatest depth to which a submarine has submerged? (a) 7.25km (4.5 miles) (b) 8km (5 miles) (c) 11km (6.8 miles)

130. Name the two collaborators on the Galileo satellite navigation system.

Grade: Hard tack

131. What is 'boxing the compass'?

132. Would a mariner use an astrolabe to establish: (a) A ship's speed (b) The position of the Milky Way (c) A ship's latitude?

133. Who invented the first doubly reflecting navigation instrument: (a) Isaac Newton (b) Galileo (c) Leonardo da Vinci?

134. What is a soldier's wind?

135. How many blades did William Froude's test propeller have: (a) One (b) Two (c) Three?

136. Where can you find the second highest tidal range in the world: (a) The Bristol Channel, between England and Wales (b) The English Channel, between France and England (c) The North Channel, between north-eastern Ireland and south-western Scotland?

137. What is the Russian equivalent of the USA's GPS: (a) GLONASS (b) GLASNOS (c) GLOSSNOSS?

138. Who first suggested seismic activity as a cause of tsunamis: (a) Pliny the Elder (b) Thucydides (c) Archimedes?

139. What was the Denny Tank used for?

140. What is the weight attached to an anchor chain to improve hold on a sailing boat called: (a) A cherub (b) A sprite (c) An angel?

Grade: Hard tack

141. What was the purpose of HMS *Beagle*'s first voyage: (a) A hydrographic survey in South America (b) A study of whale migration in South America (c) An investigation of the theory of evolution?

142. What was the caliber of Japan's Type 94 naval gun, the largest used in World War II: (a) 40cm (16in) (b) 60cm (24in) (c) 115cm (45in)?

143. What is another name for a claw anchor: (a) Brute anchor (b) Bruce anchor (c) Brace anchor?

144. What is a Great Circle route?

145. Patented in 1821, what piece of equipment had a better holding-power-to-weight ratio than what it replaced?

146. When was the first functioning Navstar GPS satellite launched: (a) 1978 (b) 1988 (c) 1998?

147. What might you learn from a bathymetric chart?

148. What is 'going over the hump' in a hovercraft?

149. What name is given to an occasional small cloud over the coast of East Africa that is a prelude to a violent wind and storm: (a) Bull's eye (b) Ox-eye (c) Bird's nest?

150. How was a chronometer used?

Grade: Hard tack

151. What sound signals should a boat under tow give in fog?

152. How much has the global mean sea level risen over the last century: (a) 2.5–7.6cm (1–3in) (b) 10–20cm (4–8in) (c) 38–51cm (15–20in)?

153. What is a crab claw sail?

154. Who used overlapping clinker boards to construct their famous vessels?

155. What is the name given to the amount by which the stern and bow rise above the level of the top deck (a) Sheer (b) Chine (c) Catena?

156. What sort of weather can you expect if you see a lunar halo?

157. What is the name of the optical instrument that creates an exact line of sight to a distant object: (a) An adelaide (b) An alidade (c) An alignaid?

158. On a steamship, what is a mack: (a) A combined smokestack and mast (b) A short mast (c) A type of anchor?

159. What is apparent wind?

160. What term describes determining the position of a boat solely by measuring distances from other points: (a) Trilation (b) Trilateration (c) Triangulation?

Grade: Able Seaman

1. How many square-rigged masts does a brig have: (a) One (b) Two (c) Three?

2. What are sailors referring to when they say the 'oggin'?

3. If someone tells you 'the rabbit comes out of the hole, around the tree and back into the hole', what are you being taught to do?

4. 'Make way' aboard a ship means: (a) Move out of my way (b) Move ahead (c) Make waves?

5. What is another name for the International Load Line?

6. What does the Blue Peter or P flag mean: (a) Ship is about to sail and all persons should report on board (b) Ship is now controlled by pirates (c) Ship is owned by the Portuguese?

7. What's the origin of the word 'halyard': (a) 'Haul yardarm' – time to anchor for the evening (b) 'Haul yards' – haul up the spar on the big sails (c) 'Haul hard' – all men on deck

8. Which race held every August is 608 nautical miles: (a) Fastnet Race (b) Fastyacht Race (c) Vendee Globe?

9. What is a derrick: (a) A spar fixed on board a ship used for hoisting cargo (b) Gallows on boats (c) A huge double anchor?

10. Name the oldest active sailing vessel in the world: (a) *Star of India* (b) *Lady Neptune* (c) *Oceana*?

Grade: Able Seaman

11. What do sailors celebrate at 'sixteen bells' time?

12. What happened on 15 April 1912?

13. What is the English abbreviation for an Unterseeboot ?

14. Which country was the first to employ submarines in war in World War I?

15. What is rhyming slang for being on the Moby Dick?

16. What is 'live ballast'?

17. What does the acronym COLREGS stand for?

18. What do the initials RMS stand for?

19. When was the sextant invented:
(a) Mid-17th century (b) Mid-18th century (c) Mid-19th century?

20. Which pirate of the Caribbean owns the luxury motor yacht *Vajoliroja*?

Did you know?

Ahoy matey! International Talk Like a Pirate Day, held on 19 September each year, was invented by Cap'n Slappy and Ol' Chumbucket.

Grade: Able Seaman

21. What is the unit of cable length named after?

22. How many cable lengths make up a nautical mile: (a) Four (b) Eight (c) Ten?

23. Where is the world's largest marine sanctuary: (a) Hawaiian Islands (b) West Indies (c) Phoenix Islands?

24. What is the name of the type of classic Chinese sailing vessel using bamboo battens?

25. Why would you not want to marry the gunner's daughter?

26. How many masts and sails does a catboat have: (a) One mast, one sail (b) One mast, two sails (c) Two masts, two sails?

27. Name the oldest naval vessel still afloat: (a) USS *Constitution* (b) HMS *Victory* (c) USS *Constellation*.

28. What does to 'chaffer up' mean in nautical slang: (a) To smarten or tidy up (b) To eat rations quickly (c) To sober up?

29. If you were introduced to a 'three-ringer', who would you be talking to? (a) A commander (b) A pirate (c) A ship's cat?

30. Which was the only vessel to return safely to Plymouth Sound after Sir Francis Drake's expedition?

Grade: Able Seaman

31. How many masts does a yawl have:
(a) One (b) Two (c) Three?

32. Which Greek god gave the Atlantic its name?

33. Which US TV series was set on a cruise ship?

34. What does IMO stand for in the nautical field?

35. What was the type of vessel known as a Balener used for:
(a) Whaling (b) Pirating (c) Sea warfare?

36. Name a slang word for the sea beginning with 'd'.

37. Where is the taffrail on a boat – bow or stern?

38. Name the ancient oared warship with two decks of oars.

39. What happened to Blackbeard's head when he died:
(a) It was cut off and suspended from the bow of First Lieutenant Maynard's sloop (b) It was cut off and thrown into the sea (c) It was cut off and embalmed as a warning to others?

40. What does 'Avast, me hearties' mean in pirate speak:
(a) 'Fire on the enemy' (b) 'Stop, and listen to me'
(c) 'Move forward now'?

Grade: Able Seaman

41. What is the Blue Riband award: (a) An unofficial award for the fastest crossing of the Atlantic Ocean (b) A trophy for the fastest crossing of the English Channel (c) An award for the fastest crossing from Florida to the Bahamas?

42. Who is the Greek god of the west wind: (a) Zephyrus (b) Boreas (c) Notus?

43. Why did ships carry false funnels in World War I and II: (a) To speed their journey (b) To disguise their outline (c) To hide weapons?

44. Who or what are Joeys in a nautical context?

45. What does the Spanish phrase El Niño mean: (a) Christ child (b) High wind (c) Virgin Mary?

46. If you are careening your ship what are you doing?

47. If you were invited to meet the Captain's daughter aboard ship, should you accept?

48. If you're having a 'kagg' in naval slang, will you be: (a) Drinking (b) Arguing (c) Eating?

49. How many dives were involved in the excavation of the *Mary Rose*: (a) 200 (b) 10,000 (c) 28,000?

50. How many times in a row is the mayday call given?

Grade: Able Seaman

51. What does the Latin word 'carina' mean?

52. What sort of cat used to be 'let out of the bag' on a ship?

53. Is a sea cucumber an animal, mineral or vegetable?

54. What would you do with 'Nelson's blood'?

55. What are 'ackers' in nautical slang:
(a) Foreign currency (b) Inedible rations (c) Shipmates?

56. From what city does the term 'lagoon' originate?

57. Where is the Britannia Royal Naval College situated:
(a) Plymouth, UK (b) Portsmouth, UK (c) Dartmouth, UK?

58. Where was the RMS *Titanic* built:
(a) New York, USA (b) Glasgow, Scotland (c) Belfast, Northern Ireland?

59. Sir Arthur Conan Doyle wrote a short story based on the mysterious fate of a ship called *Amazon*; what was the vessel renamed?

60. How many days did the *Mayflower* take to make the Atlantic crossing in 1620: (a) 42 (b) 50 (c) 66?

Did you know?

Blackbeard had 40 cannons on his pirate ship, *Queen Anne's Revenge*.

Grade: Midshipman

61. How long did Darwin's voyage on HMS *Beagle* last: (a) Almost two years (b) Almost five years (c) Almost seven years?

62. Which Irish rock star owns the superyacht *Cyan*?

63. What does 'chatty' mean in nautical slang: (a) Dirty or untidy (b) Uncommunicative (c) Noisy?

64. Who crooned 'True Love' to Grace Kelly on board a yacht in the filmed version of *High Society*?

65. Which gaff-rigged vessel won the inaugural Fastnet Race in 1925 and twice more?

66. Which ship do some people claim ignored the distress signals of RMS *Titanic*?

67. Which 'challenger' beat which 'defender' in the 1983 America's Cup?

68. What is the name of the British royal family's yacht, decommissioned in 1997?

69. What musical purpose was the refitted Danish passenger ferry *Fredericia* used for in 1964?

70. What is the difference between clinker planking and carvel planking in hulls?

Grade: Midshipman

71. One of Christopher Columbus's ships was called *Pinta*; what does the word mean?

72. John Denver wrote a modern sea shanty as a tribute to his friend Jacques Cousteau and his research ship – name that tune.

73. Which of these items were used by Cornelius Drebbel to submerge his submarine: (a) Pigs' bladders (b) Balloons (c) Ballast?

74. Where on a ship would you find a skyscraper?

75. Which transatlantic liner was known as 'the grand old lady of the Atlantic': (a) RMS *Mauretania* (b) RMS *Lusitania* (c) RMS *Titanic*?

76. 'Wigs and hairpieces must not present a safety or FOD hazard.' What is FOD in this context: (a) Foreign Object Damage (b) Foreign Object Debris (c) Fashion Order Directive?

77. Which food does the slang expression 'black-coated workers' refer to?

78. Where is the British clipper, the *Cutty Sark*, preserved?

79. In the US Navy what does FTN officially stand for: (a) Fighting Temporary Navy (b) Forget the Navy (c) Full-time Navy?

80. What are you doing if you 'swallow the anchor': (a) Getting drunk (b) Refusing to set sail (c) Retiring from sea life and settling down ashore?

Grade: Midshipman

81. The practice of hoisting false flags to deceive enemies is the origin of a commonly used word. Is it: (a) Befuddle (b) Bamboozle (c) Bemuse?

82. Which ocean liner split HMS *Curacoa* in two in October 1942?

83. Which Australian actor from Hollywood's golden age owned two yachts named *Sirocco*?

84. What are 'honkydonks' in nautical slang: (a) Drinking games created by Royal Marines (b) A sailor's name for shoes worn by Royal Marines for shore service (c) Sea shanties sung in the 19th century?

85. What does the old naval term 'banyan party' mean?

86. How many lives were lost on RMS *Lusitania*: (a) 452 (b) 785 (c) 1,198?

87. Which lighthouse was one of the Seven Wonders of the World?

88. Which country has won the most Olympic medals in sailing events (up till and including 2012): (a) USA (b) Britain (c) Australia?

89. What is the other name for a Bermuda rig: (a) California rig (b) Marconi rig (c) Somers rig?

90. Name the type of sailing boat from the USA in the 1850s which used sandbags as moveable ballast: (a) Sandbagger (b) Sandlugger (c) Sand-dragger.

Grade: Midshipman

91. Which drummer from an iconic 1960s' pop group drowned at Marina Del Rey, Los Angeles, in 1983, and was buried at sea?

92. Who was rescued from his overturned hull of *Exide Challenger* in the Southern Ocean in 1996?

93. What is a yawkyawk: (a) A pregnant whale in Aboriginal mythology (b) A large albatross-like bird in Aboriginal mythology (c) A female character similar to a mermaid in Aboriginal mythology?

94. Which World War I poet died on board a French hospital ship: (a) Wilfrid Owen (b) Rupert Brooke (c) Siegfried Sassoon?

95. In which country was the fifie type of sailing boat developed (a) Ireland (b) Norway (c) Scotland?

96. Are 'canteen medals' on your jacket things to be proud of?

97. What are 'beetle crushers' in nautical slang?

98. On the Plimsoll Line, what do the letters TF mean?

99. If you are 'over the barrel' in nautical slang, are you: a) About to be sick b) Hopelessly drunk c) In a weak position?

100. In which year was the first international sailing race held between the USA and the UK: (a) 1801 (b) 1851 (c) 1891?

Grade: Midshipman

101. Name one of the southern coast towns in the UK that used to be a Cinque Port in medieval times.

102. Which landlocked country won the America's Cup in 2003 and 2007?

103. What is a more local word for Greenwich Mean Time (GMT): (a) Zulu time (b) Amazon time (c) London time?

104. Where is a replica of HMS *Beagle* being constructed: (a) The Historic Dockyard, Portsmouth, England (b) The Nao Victoria Museum, Punta Arenas, Chile (c) The Royal Navy Base, Clyde, Scotland?

105. On the passenger list of which boat did Bob Hope, Salvador Dali, Rita Hayworth, Duke Ellington and the Duke and Duchess of Windsor all appear in the 1950s?

106. What was Thor Heyerdahl's *Kon-Tiki* raft made of?

107. What colour flag do you fly to indicate the owner is absent: (a) Red (b) White (c) Blue?

108. Which naval phrase is thought to be the origin of 'posh'?

109. Who took part in the ill-fated 1968 Golden Globe Race aboard *Teignmouth Electron*?

110. If you have scrambled egg on your peaked cap, should you be proud or embarrassed?

Grade: Midshipman

111. How many lives were lost on RMS *Titanic*: (a) 758 (b) 972 (c) 1,503?

112. What is another name for the America's Cup: (a) Auld Mug (b) Auld Lang (c) Big Old?

113. What are 'mundungus' in nautical slang: (a) Useless sailors (b) Useless commanders (c) Useless bits of material?

114. What type of vessel was Captain James Cook's ship *Endeavour*: (a) Whitby collier (b) Cumbrian carrack (c) Scarborough sloop?

115. Which US black activist said: 'We may have all come on different ships, but we're in the same boat now.'?

116. Who said: 'There is plenty of time to win this game, and to thrash the Spaniards too.'?

117. Which publishing mogul is presumed to have fallen overboard from his yacht *Lady Ghislaine* in 1991?

118. Which scandalous royal rendezvous occurred aboard the *Nahlin* in the 1930s?

119. How many days did the *Mayflower II* take to make an Atlantic crossing in 1957: (a) 53 (b) 65 (c) 78?

120. Which pilot cutter was the overall winner of the Tall Ships Race in 2000 and 2002?

Grade: Hard tack

121. Which sailing trophy did London jeweller Robert Garrard design?

122. Which Greek goddess was carved out of which special wood on the *Argo*?

123. How deep is the water when someone shouts 'Mark Twain': (a) One fathom (1.8m/6ft) (b) Two fathoms (3.7m/12ft) (c) Three fathoms (5.5m/18ft)?

124. What was the proper name of 'Bogie's Boat'?

125. Which country hosted the Olympic and Paralympic Sailing competitions in 2008?

126. Where did the MS *Estonia* sink in 1994: (a) The North Sea (b) The Baring Sea (c) The Baltic Sea?

127. Which race, sponsored by a multinational energy company, was inspired by the Golden Globe Race?

128. Which female Hollywood star drowned on a weekend boat trip off the coast of California in 1981?

129. What is the name of Rod Stewart's famous album of 1975 on which 'I am Sailing' appears?

130. What happened to RMS *Carpathia* in 1917?

Grade: Hard tack

131. Who invented the first automated foghorn in the mid-19th century: (a) Robert Foulis (b) Richard Fogle (c) Ronald Foundhorn?

132. The wreck of a 14th-century BCE trading vessel found in 1982 in Turkey is known as: (a) The Uluburun (b) The Bodrum (c) The Çakir?

133. What is the name of the 55m (180ft) luxury boat once owned by Rupert Murdoch: (a) *Rosemary* (b) *Rosehearty* (c) *Lady Rose*?

134. Which year was the maiden voyage of the SS *United States*: (a) 1952 b) 1962 c) 1972?

135. Which British entrepreneur and inventor of household appliances is the current owner of *Nahlin*?

136. Where did HMS *Beagle* end her days: (a) As a working vessel in Tierra del Fuego (b) As a coastguard ship on the Essex coast in the UK (c) In a dockyard in Patagonia after restoration?

137. Which famous Welsh actor bought the *Kalizma* for his equally famous wife in 1967?

138. If you were a rosewater sailor in the 19th century, were you: (a) On shore leave (b) High-achieving (c) An incompetent officer?

139. On which European river does the Lorelei's music lure in sailors to their death: (a) The Danube (b) The Elba (c) The Rhine?

140. Name the oldest yacht club in Russia (founded early 18th century).

Grade: Hard tack

141. Which team from the US won the America's Cup in 2013?

142. What was the name of the daily newspaper on RMS *Titanic*: (a) *Atlantic Daily Bulletin* (b) *Atlantic Daily Gazette* (c) *Titanic Mail*?

143. In which Olympic Games did sailing races first take place: (a) 1896 (b) 1900 (c) 1908?

144. Which famous UK author of detective novels sailed on whaling ship SS *Hope* to the Arctic as a medical officer in 1880?

145. What is the name of the superyacht designed by Philippe Starck for the late Steve Jobs and unveiled after his death: (a) *Neptune* (b) *Mercury* (c) *Venus*?

146. Where was the SS *Deutschland* headed in 1875 when she ran aground and who was on board?

147. In which year did the inaugural BOC Challenge race take place: (a) 1982 (b) 1992 (c) 2002?

148. Which English queen changed the name of the warship *Ark Raleigh* to *Ark Royal*?

149. Which US passenger liner was Leroy J Alexanderson the last captain of?

150. Which renowned navigational astronomer lost part of his nose in a duel over a mathematical formula with a Danish nobleman?

Grade: Hard tack

151. In heraldry, what does an anchor represent: (a) Salvation, hope and religious steadfastness (b) The power of the sea (c) Faith, hope and charity?

152. Which clipper won the Great Tea Race of 1866?

153. Which French expression does the word 'mayday' come from?

154. Which 19th-century English writer said: 'We are all in the same boat, on a stormy sea, and we owe each other a terrible loyalty'?

155. What was the name of the first commercially successful steamboat on the Hudson River in the USA, in 1807: (a) *The Hudson Hopper* (b) *The Clermont* (c) *The Fairwind Fortune*?

156. The Barthel trophy is awarded to the winner of which yachting challenge established in 2001 in the USA?

157. Name one (or two!) of the largest private sailing yachts in the world.

158. What struck the coast of Cornwall on 1 November 1755, having travelled over 1,600km (995 miles) in four hours?

159. The yacht *Al Mansur* (The Victor) was bombed by Tomcats from USS *Constellation* in 2003; who did it belong to: (a) Muammar Al-Qaddafi (b) Saddam Hussein (c) King Jong-il?

160. Which coast is being raced to in the Race to the Coast, the oldest point-to-point regatta in the western hemisphere?

Grade: Able Seaman

1. Right side of a vessel as you look forward
2. Left side of a vessel as you look forward
3. Forwardmost part of a vessel
4. Aftmost part of a vessel
5. Marine latrine
6. Kitchen area of a vessel
7. The watertight body of a vessel
8. Tiller or wheel
9. Number of feet in a fathom
10. Padding between vessels to prevent damage

Did you know?

The name 'crew neck' for a style of collar comes from the types of shirts traditionally worn by oarsmen.

Grade: Able Seaman

11. Sudden, violent wind accompanied by rain

12. Bar or handle for turning rudder or outboard motor

13. Collective term for anchor and mooring gear

14. Opposite of ahead

15. Boarding accessway

16. To put items in proper place

17. Direction a vessel's bow points

18. Depth of water a vessel draws

19. A vessel's greatest width

20. To revolt against the captain

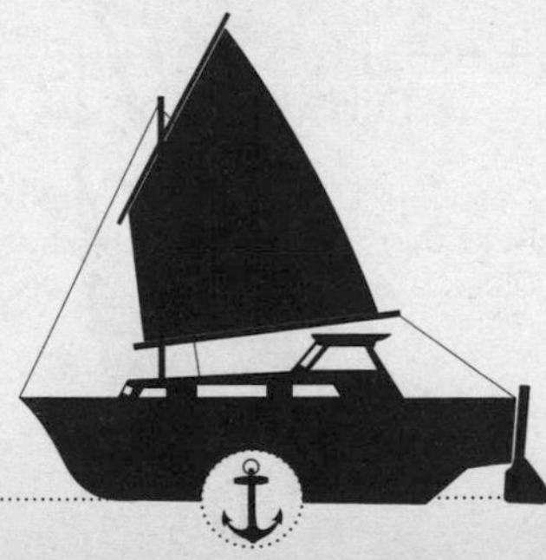

Grade: Able Seaman

21. The waves made by a passing vessel

22. Command to stop doing something

23. A float moored by a jetty or vessel

24. Unable to move through lack of wind

25. A shore downwind of a vessel

26. Two successive half-hitches

27. A person who carries a jinx

28. One nautical mile per hour

29. To roll up a sail tightly

30. A loop in a rope or line

Grade: Able Seaman

31. The upper edges of a vessel's sides

32. A trespasser on a vessel

33. A long, thin triangular flag

34. Fitting to secure a line without a knot

35. One minute of arc of latitude

36. A bracket to hold an oar

37. The forward edge of a sail

38. Rope used to set a sail to the wind

39. The stand for a compass

40. Command just before tacking

Did you know?

Ancraophobia is the name given to the condition of extreme fear of wind or draft.

THE ANSWERS

Geography

P4

1. Northern Canada
2. (a) Bristol, England
3. (c) Atlantic Ocean
4. Sirocco
5. Bay of Biscay and the Mediterranean Sea
6. (a) Annapolis, Maryland
7. It's a maelstrom off the coast of Norway in the Lofoten Islands
8. South Africa
9. (b) Cuba
10. (c) Shanghai

P5

11. A device for measuring wind speed
12. Belgium
13. Port Said
14. The Falkland Islands
15. Jamestown, Virginia
16. South of mainland South America and north of Tierra del Fuego
17. Strong westerly winds found in the southern hemisphere
18. North Atlantic
19. Cowes, Isle of Wight, UK
20. Indonesia

P6

21. Newfoundland
22. The Caribbean Sea
23. Panama Canal
24. The Mistral
25. Between the Tropic of Cancer and the Arctic Circle in the north, and between the Tropic of Capricorn and the Antarctic Circle in the south
26. Hudson River, New York State, USA
27. Prince William Sound, Alaska
28. Pacific, Atlantic, Indian, Southern and Arctic oceans
29. The Gulf Stream
30. Lisbon, Portugal

P7

31. The Canary Islands
32. A light breeze, Beaufort Scale 2
33. (b) Greenland
34. The Suez Canal
35. Christmas Island
36. (a) Sydney Harbour
37. (b) The Red Sea
38. It is the saltiest lake in the world and the lowest point on Earth
39. A row of three distinctive stacks of chalk off the coast of the Isle of Wight, UK
40. South Africa

P8

41. (c) The Sea of Marmara (between the Aegean and Black seas in Turkey)
42. (b) Canada
43. Marseille
44. Venice, Italy
45. Japanese (it means 'harbour wave')
46. (a) Seven
47. Next to the shore
48. San Francisco
49. Intertropical Convergence Zone
50. A strong tide that pushes up a river, against the current

P9

51. In the Atlantic Ocean (about 965km/600 miles west of Portugal)
52. Porto
53. Liberty Island, New York Harbour
54. Russia and the USA
55. The Mediterranean Sea
56. Largest to smallest: Superior, Huron, Michigan, Erie, Ontario
57. Seas are smaller than oceans and usually located where land and ocean meet. Seas are typically partially enclosed by land
58. To the right (or clockwise)
59. St Petersburg
60. A band of warm ocean water found periodically off the west coast of South America (most noticeable around Christmas)

P10

61. The Challenger Deep in the Mariana Trench (est. 11,033m/36,198ft)
62. (c) Southampton Water
63. (c) The British Isles and the Atlantic coast of Europe
64. (b) Port of Trieste, Italy
65. In the southern hemisphere between latitudes 50° and 60° (they are strong westerly winds)
66. Cape Town, South Africa
67. For its calm, peaceful waters
68. (c) The Weddell Sea
69. (a) Taiwan
70. Southampton, UK, Cherbourg, France, Queenstown (Cobh), Ireland

P11

71. Gibraltar
72. Bruges
73. The Northwest Passage
74. (b) A sandbank at the mouth of the Thames Estuary
75. The South China Sea
76. The Susquehanna River
77. Madeira
78. In the Straits of Florida, north of Cuba
79. (c) Cape Agulhas
80. Lock-type canal

P12

81. (a) Along the narrow fjords of British Columbia, Canada
82. Nile (6,650km/4,132 miles), Amazon (6,400km/3,976 miles), Yangtze (6,300km/3,917 miles)
83. Stockholm, Sweden
84. Hamburg, Germany
85. Bristol; an area of tidal river that allows ships to remain afloat all the time
86. 155 million square kilometres (59 million square miles)
87. (c) Port Elizabeth
88. In the tropics, where they make up the prevailing easterly surface winds
89. (c) 27m (90ft)
90. The Sargasso Sea, located entirely in the Atlantic Ocean

P13

91. Levanter
92. (a) Bay of Fundy, Canada (about 17m (56ft)

93. A portable temporary concrete harbour used by the Allies in World War II
94. Portugal
95. The Kingdom of the Netherlands (they are Aruba, Bonaire and Curaçao)
96. The Gulf of Mexico
97. Cape of Storms (Cabo des Tormentas)
98. Between Cape Horn in South America and Antarctica
99. Grigale (Gregale)
100. In Lisbon, Portugal, under the Vasco da Gama Bridge, built in 1998

P14

101. The Azores
102. The Port of Split, Croatia
103. (b) Persian Gulf
104. Lake Titicaca in the Andes between Peru and Bolivia
105. It's not actually a sea, it's a lake
106. (c) The Port of New York and New Jersey
107. (b) Admiralty Building, St Petersburg
108. (a) Bohemia
109. Honolulu, Hawaii
110. (c) Exeter

P15

111. The highest tsunami ever recorded
112. Weymouth, Dorset, UK
113. (b) New Zealand
114. A powerful katabatic north-easterly wind affecting the Adriatic Sea
115. (c) Sicily
116. Ships would sail from Europe to a latitude around the Azores or the Canaries (at which point the temperature is warm enough to melt butter); here they could turn west and benefit from the northeast trade winds on their passage while avoiding the westerly depressions that come in from the ocean to the north
117. The 'high water' that regularly floods the port and city of Venice, Italy
118. Moderate waves of some length, many whitecaps and small amounts of spray
119. (b) More than 7,000
120. Two – the Chesapeake Bay Bridge in Maryland and the Chesapeake Bay Bridge-Tunnel in Virginia

P16

121. Two square red flags with a black square at the centre of each
122. Newfoundland (Cape Bonavista)
123. (b) 170
124. Fortunate weather encountered by the British Navy of the 16th–17th centuries, starting with the storm that destroyed the Spanish Armada in 1588
125. To South America; a circumnavigation of the earth; and a final expedition to Australia
126. The Cape of Good Hope
127. Lake Baikal in Siberia, Russia. It is 1,637m (5,369ft) deep – more than one mile straight down

128. Tallinn, Estonia
129. Wellington Harbour. Poneke is a transliteration of Port Nick; Port Nicholson is the city's central area
130. From the east coast of Taiwan past Japan towards the North Pacific

P17

131. Between August 1803 and August 1806, under the leadership of Adam Johann von Krusenstern
132. The Virgin Islands
133. (b) Eight
134. Across the Mediterranean from the south-east, onto the French Languedoc and Roussillon coast
135. The Java Sea and the Indian Ocean
136. China, Burma, Laos, Thailand, Cambodia, Vietnam
137. Charlotte Amalie, named after the wife of King Christian V of Denmark
138. A ring-shaped coral reef including a coral rim that encircles a lagoon partially or completely
139. (b) The Port of Vancouver
140. The Baltic, around the Frisian Islands

P18

141. Cape of Good Hope, Cape Leeuwin, South East Cape, South West Cape, Cape Horn
142. Ceuta, North Africa
143. (a) A kamal
144. The Volga, Russia (3,962km/ 2,294 miles)
145. Labrador current
146. Near the modern-day Bahamas; they named the island San Salvador
147. Through La Paz, Mexico, named after the British sailor Samuel Cromwell
148. The English Channel
149. The South China Sea
150. (c) Commonwealth Bay, Antarctica

P19

151. On the Fujita scale from F0 (weakest) to F5 (strongest)
152. Cape Coral, Florida
153. Southend Pier
154. (c) China (although some theories suggest parts of Central America)
155. From Peru to American Samoa, a distance of 10,780km (6,700 miles)
156. It's the Caribbean Sea and the Gulf of Mexico combined
157. The South China Sea – it's an atoll of reefs and shoals otherwise known as the Zhongsha Islands
158. Saba, Sint Maarten and Sint Eustatius in the Lesser Antilles in the Caribbean Sea
159. The Indian Ocean, with a seismic epicentre off the west coast of Sumatra, Indonesia
160. Stamford, Connecticut, USA from the yacht club to Buzzards Bay and back

Famous people

P20

1. Italian
2. Asia, by sailing around Africa to India
3. (c) Naval advisor
4. Portugal
5. Admiral Lord Nelson, born at Burnham Thorpe
6. President John F Kennedy and Jackie Onassis
7. Blackbeard
8. Ferdinand Magellan and Sir Francis Drake
9. Fastest woman to single-handedly circumnavigate the globe non-stop
10. Charles Darwin

P21

11. Sir Edward Heath
12. Being the first to introduce potatoes and tobacco. They were actually first brought to Europe by the Spanish
13. Captain James Cook
14. Sir Chay Blyth
15. A pirate
16. Aristotle Onassis
17. Portuguese
18. Tasmania (named in 1856)
19. He was captain of the *Bounty* when the sailors mutinied in 1789
20. The Royal National Lifeboat Institution (RNLI)

P22

21. (b) Seven
22. Davy Jones has been an evil spirit, pirate or ghost personified. The meaning is death at the bottom of the sea
23. 'England expects that every man shall do his duty'
24. Ferdinand Magellan
25. Captain Edward Smith
26. Jeremy Irons
27. (c) Captain James Cook
28. The marine chronometer, used for determining longitude at sea
29. (a) Just over 78 days
30. Sir Francis Chichester

P23

31. (a) Mrs Chippy
32. Captain William Kidd
33. Fletcher Christian
34. Captain Henry Morgan
35. The scale of wind force
36. Admiral Lord Nelson
37. Commander of the pirate ship *The Walrus* in *Treasure Island* by Robert Louis Stevenson
38. Kaines Adlard Coles
39. Benjamin Franklin
40. (a) Dame Naomi James

P24

41. His right arm
42. HMS *Beagle*
43. (c) Caligula
44. Sir Ben Ainslie
45. Dame Ellen MacArthur
46. *Endurance*
47. At 16, she was was the youngest sailor to circumnavigate the world single-handedly
48. (a) John Franklin
49. Chay Blyth and John Ridgway
50. Mary Read and Anne Bonny

P25

51. The Plimsoll Line on ships' hulls indicating maximum safe draft
52. Paul Elvstrom
53. John Lennon
54. The Virgin Mary (also known as the 'Mystic Rose') or Mary Tudor
55. Sir Francis Chichester
56. Sir Humphrey Bogart (the race is called the Bogart series)
57. Robin Lee Graham
58. At the Battle of Trafalgar in 1805
59. Andrew Simpson
60. (c) 30,123

P26

61. They rescued survivors from British coastal steamer SS *Forfarshire* in 1838
62. (b) First person to solo circumnavigate the globe twice
63. *The Weather Book*
64. The *Mayflower*
65. He had to turn back on 15 November due to contrary winds and set off again on 13 December
66. Sir Winston Churchill
67. Dawn Riley
68. Isoroko Yamamoto
69. (a) The first navigable submarine
70. Sir Ernest Shackleton

P27

71. King William IV
72. Thomas Andrews
73. Captain Benjamin Briggs
74. *Fram*
75. She was the first woman to sail solo across the Atlantic
76. Leif Ericson, son of Erik the Red
77. Francis Joyon
78. Sir Richard Branson
79. Sir Peter Blake
80. (a) The first African-American to sail solo around the world

P28

81. (a) John Rackham
82. Draco
83. He built a boat called the *Ra*
84. Joshua Slocum
85. The Duke of Medina Sidonia and the Duke of Parma
86. (b) Violet Jessop
87. Alex Thomson
88. Andrew Cunningham
89. Sean Connery
90. Tracy Edwards

P29

91. A new world sailing speed record (65.45 knots)
92. (a) Commodore Harry Manning
93. Vasco da Gama
94. (a) Chester W Nimitz
95. *Ice Bird*
96. Samuel Pepys
97. Josiah Wedgwood II
98. Jeanne Socrates
99. Captain John Paul Jones
100. The record for the women's westwards single-handed non-stop sailing around the world

P30

101. The attack on Pearl Harbor
102. The Atlantic
103. (a) Adrian Flanagan
104. She was North America's first registered female sea captain
105. *Nina* and *Pinta*
106. (a) President John F Kennedy
107. *Kon-Tiki*
108. *Virgin Atlantic Challenger II*
109. Fletcher Christian
110. (a) In the Philippines, at the hands of local tribesmen on the island of Mactan

P31

111. Raold Amundsen
112. Silver
113. Captain James Cook
114. Percy Bysshe Shelley
115. Alex Thomson
116. Morgan Freeman
117. Ida Zorada Lewis, who saved many lives at Lime Rock lighthouse, Rhode Island
118. (a) Admiral Sir Cloudesley Shovell
119. Dame Ellen MacArthur
120. Jessica Watson

P32

121. Jonas Hogh-Christensen
122. ABC
123. (a) Alain Thébault
124. Fleet Admiral Ernest Joseph King
125. (a) A man
126. Bernard Moitessier
127. (a) John White
128. She was the first black female sailor, disguised as a man
129. Admiral George Anson
130. Rear Admiral Lillian Elaine Fishburne

P33

131. Dennis Conner
132. (a) The Argentine
133. (a) Japan
134. John Cabot
135. The sea wolf ('Le loup des mers')
136. All three!
137. Mike Golding
138. Sir Francis Drake's sword
139: (a) Captain Philip Roberts
140. Sir Walter Raleigh

P34

141. Pete Goss on *Aqua Quorum* rescued Raphael Dinelli
142. In a failed attack on Charleston, South Carolina
143. *QE2*
144. They were among the 69 sledge dogs on board
145. Bartholomew Roberts
146. Adolf Hitler
147. Éric Tabarly
148. Easter Island
149. (a) SS *Deutschland*
150. Dawn Riley

P35

151. (a) Michel Desjoyeaux
152. Giovanni da Verrazano
153. Roz Savage
154. Mylene Pacquette from Montreal
155. Crispin Money-Coutts
156. Amelia Erhart
157. Vito Dumas
158. At the Battle of Cape Lopez, off what is now Gabon, West Africa, in 1722
159. Chay Blyth
160. Admiral Sir Dudley Pound

History

P36

1. The Vikings
2. (b) An elevated structure at the stern
3. Greeks, Phoenicians, Romans
4. Dugout canoe
5. 'Broadside' is used to describe all three
6. *Torrey Canyon*
7. (b) 1519
8. Bell-bottom (wide) trousers
9. Off the coast of Portsmouth, UK
10. HMS *Victory*

P37

11. Three
12. The paddle wheel
13. By oars
14. SS *Great Britain*
15. She was torpedoed by a German U-boat
16. A wooden lighthouse
17. A drink made with water (or occasionally weak beer) and rum
18. The bubonic plague
19. Bows (it was used as a platform for archers)
20. 'Old Ironsides', Boston, Massachusetts, USA

P38

21. (b) Tea
22. (c) Lisbon, Portugal
23. Salted and stored in barrels
24. A young boy who kept the gun crews supplied with gunpowder
25. Press-gang
26. A barge for transferring goods and passengers to and from moored ships
27. A prolongation of the bow underwater, to drive into the hull of an enemy ship
28. In a cask filled with brandy

29. *Rainbow Warrior*
30. Death or transportation to the colonies

P39

31. An iron-plated warship powered by steam
32. White Star Line
33. (b) An aircraft carrier
34. Convicts
35. (b) Traditionally, a ship with the captain's wife on board
36. (c) The Thames, London, UK
37. Ship's biscuit, mainly made of flour
38. (a) Floating prisons
39. (b) Ran the gauntlet of the crew armed with knotted ropes
40. (b) Baltimore clipper

P40

41. Ships were formed in a single line so that no ship masked another when firing a broadside
42. 18 men
43. Nothing, it was just for show
44. A barrel or basket
45. (b) Mess
46. (b) Sea chests containing their personal possessions
47. The America's Cup
48. (a) Caligula
49. (a) The Arabs
50. (c) *Yongala*

P41

51. A warship
52. RMS *Carpathia*
53. By a horse walking along a canal towpath
54. World War I
55. (b) Four
56. Oil, such as whale or vegetable oil
57. The Dreadnought
58. Argentinian
59. One sail
60. (a) Combustible material used to set fire to enemy ships

P42

61. (a) 8 knots (15 km/h)
62. (a) Battle of Leyte Gulf
63. France
64. English settlers (who founded Jamestown, Virginia)
65. Cunard Line
66. Newfoundland
67. Australia
68. (c) 4,000
69. Around 5,000 calories
70. US cargo ships, in World War II

P43

71. The lateen sail
72. The Battle of Jutland in 1916
73. Supposedly at Tilbury, Essex
74. (b) 160km (100 miles)
75. An apprentice officer (similar to today's petty officer)
76. (a) A Dutch and Flemish fishing boat for catching herring
77. (c) Carvel
78. (a) Antony and Cleopatra's
79. Adze
80. (c) 1580

P44

81. (a) *Preussen*
82. To India and back
83. A small three-masted, fully rigged warship
84. (b) William Kidd
85. (c) Portugal
86. A single square sail
87. Warships were powered by oars, merchant ships by sail
88. HMS *Victory*
89. A whaling ship
90. (a) 1844

P45

91. The lowest deck on a sailing warship
92. Landing craft used in World War II
93. A submersible
94. (b) Birch
95. (a) Two or three
96. She sank after barely 1.3km (less than a mile)
97. From their role of cruising and scouting for enemy fleets
98. Animal hide stretched across a wicker or wooden frame
99. Pearl Harbor, Hawaii; it can be viewed through the glass floor in a building above it
100. Originally the nickname given to the seamen of the British merchant and Royal navies

P46

101. She had a circular hull
102. Lloyd's, London, UK
103. They sent fire ships into the Spanish fleet to break up its formation
104. Egypt (at the Giza pyramid complex)
105. *Bismarck*
106. Yokohama harbour, Japan
107. They mutinied over maggot-infested rotten meat delivered to the ship
108. (c) 1 gallon (4.5 litres)
109. (a) North Africa
110. Alfred von Tirpitz

P47

111. The French (a branch of their foreign intelligence service)
112. Off Victoria's Shipwreck Coast, Australia
113. Store rooms, junior officers' cabins, medical bay, engine room
114. Charles II
115. Lightship
116. (c) She mysteriously disappeared without trace
117. (a) 1788
118. It was fought almost entirely with aircraft launched from aircraft carriers
119. Royal Cork Yacht Club, Ireland
120. (a) The Netherlands

P48

121. Cyprus
122. (c) The Portuguese
123. The HL *Hunley* (in the American Civil War)
124. The defeat of the Spanish Armada

125. The Greek fleet
126. Nuclear-powered submarine
127. (a) The Hebrides
128. (c) SS *Bremen*
129. Polaris missiles
130. (b) Pirates

P49

131. (b) 1982
132. They were ironclad warships, used for the first time in battle
133. (b) MV *Doña Paz* (a ferry which collided with the *Vector* in 1987 with a possible death toll of 4,375 people)
134. An ancient Greek galley powered by 50 oars
135. America's Cup (1851), Fastnet (1925), Sydney Hobart (1945)
136. Fresnel lens
137. Carthaginians and Romans
138. (a) A walkway dropped onto an enemy ship to board it
139. (a) 3300 BCE
140. It was the last great naval battle fought by galleys manned by oarsmen

P50

141. (b) 1930s
142. A warship with an upper deck covered in armour plating and spikes
143. Slaves from West Africa being transported around Cuba
144. (c) Tahiti and the Polynesian islands
145. SS *Vaterland*, German
146. HMS *Revenge*
147. (c) *Batavia*
148. She was the first North Atlantic liner with a cruiser stern, ie curving forwards rather than backwards
149. An ancient Roman lighthouse found at La Coruña in northern Spain
150. Amerigo Vespucci

P51

151. (a) A clipper
152. *Admiral Scheer*, *Deutschland*, *Admiral Graf Spee*
153. Blackbeard, aka Edward Teach
154. Nuclear submarine USS *Nautilus*
155. (b) Three
156. The schooner *America*, on the Isle of Wight, UK
157. The American Civil War
158. (c) A social meeting of the crews on board whaleships at sea
159. Henry Hudson
160. He sailed past Cape Bojador, on the northern coast of Western Sahara, thus opening up a route to the rest of Africa and eventually to India

Culture

P52

1. Errol Flynn
2. Ratty (a water rat)
3. Homer, from the *Odyssey*
4. 'There Is Nothin' Like a Dame'
5. The owl and the pussycat 'took some money and plenty of honey' in Edward Lear's nonsense rhyme
6. The attempted escape of shipwreck survivors on a raft

7. Poseidon, Neptune
8. *The Little Mermaid*
9. Alistair MacLean
10. 'And all I ask is a tall ship and a star to steer her by'

P53

11. Jimmy Cliff
12. The Hebrides, Scotland
13. A boater
14. A trident
15. A spacecraft
16. (a) A river boat
17. Benjamin Britten
18. Barry Manilow
19. *HMS Pinafore*
20. The Disneyland theme park ride of the same name

P54

21. Chanter, meaning to sing
22. Two groups of children who adopt the names of their dinghies
23. *Queen*
24. Claude Monet
25. She has short-term memory loss
26. Ernest Hemingway
27. 'To me, way hey, blow the man down'
28. Jane and Henry Fonda
29. Herman Melville's whale, Moby-Dick
30. JMW Turner

P55

31. She overturns completely in the water
32. Sydney Opera House
33. Keith Richards of *The Rolling Stones*
34. *The Police*
35. The Blue Meanies
36. *Treasure Island*
37. A small river steamboat
38. *The Phantom of the Opera*
39. Peter the Great
40. Somali

P56

41. Rod Stewart
42. Samuel Taylor Coleridge, an albatross
43. The Jolly Roger, the pirates' flag of skull and crossbones (or swords)
44. *Argo*, Jason
45. (c) Five times (1916, 1933, 1935, 1962, 1984)
46. The Mississippi River, USA
47. (a) The Thames
48. The complete melting of the polar ice caps
49. *Pequod*
50. Pacific Ocean

P57

51. 'My Heart Will Go On', Céline Dion
52. The Bayeux Tapestry
53. David Gray
54. Ratty in *Wind in the Willows*
55. A giant squid or octopus
56. The Beach Boys as 'Sloop John B'
57. The hornpipe
58. Canaletto
59. (b) US nuclear submarine
60. Enya

P58

61. Captain Flint, 'Pieces of eight!'
62. (a) *White Squall*
63. Henry Wadsworth Longfellow
64. The whaleship, *Essex*
65. 'Eternal Father, Strong to Save'
66. (c) *Grey and Green*
67. The Amazon
68. Captain Wolf Larsen
69. Claude Debussy
70. Ralph Waldo Emerson

P59

71. Crosby, Stills & Nash
72. (b) Le Havre
73. Jack Aubrey, Stephen Maturin
74. (c) *Captain Blood*
75. Miss Nancy Blair
76. Dylan Thomas
77. (a) Sir Edward Elgar
78. Cork, Ireland, bound for New York
79. The shark that ate his friend
80. CS Forester

P60

81. At the windlass or capstan ('so heave the capstan and make it spin round')
82. Joseph Conrad, *Lord Jim*
83. Alexander Selkirk
84. A postage stamp
85. Corvette, to escort convoys across the Atlantic Ocean in World War II
86. (b) Mickey Mouse
87. Captain Cook
88. A fleet of packet ships that sailed between England and America, known for their harsh conditions
89. 'A Life on the Ocean Wave'
90. The Mississippi River

P61

91. A great wave (off Kanagawa)
92. (a) New York
93. Ripley kills Dickie with an oar
94. (c) A rogue container
95. Roy Orbison
96. (b) The Congo
97. Sam Neill, Nicole Kidman, Billy Zane
98. Crossing out the names of past loves and adding a new one
99. Mark Twain
100. *The Perfect Storm*

P62

101. Rembrandt
102. Ralph Vaughan Williams
103. A father/son relationship is implied
104. Captain Nemo, *Nautilus*
105. Captain Hector Barbossa
106. (a) Lisbon
107. The Dutchman, Daland, Senta, Erik, Mary, Daland's steersman
108. Christopher Reeve
109. Ernest Hemingway
110. A many-headed serpent

P63

111. 'The Boat' in German
112. Entice fishermen with her beauty before luring them to their deaths
113. Peter Benchley

114. (c) *HMS Surprise*
115. (c) Thomas Eakins
116. Hector Berlioz
117. Charon
118. *The Ninth Wave*
119. Cary Grant, Tony Curtis
120. *Hispaniola*, named after the West Indian island, today made up of Haiti and the Dominican Republic

P64

121. (b) Charles Trenet
122. *On Stranger Tides*
123. *Scheherazade*, Nikolai Rimsky-Korsakov
124. Winslow Homer
125. It can be rendered undetectable (by a 'caterpillar drive' in the film, by a pump-jet in the novel)
126. His daughter, from 'The Wreck of the Hesperus'
127. 'Oceans'
128. Kahlil Gibran
129. George Chambers
130. Into the veins of a man

P65

131. Nick Drake
132. Edgar Allan Poe
133. He must remain apprenticed to the pirates until his 21st birthday; he is now 21 but since he was born on 29 February, his birthday only occurs every four years and so he must serve them for many more to come
134. A model of Nelson's *Victory* in a bottle by Yinka Shonibare
135. A water horse, a beautiful woman
136. The SS *Edmund Fitzgerald*, which sank in Lake Superior
137. Joshua Slocum, *Sailing Alone Around the World*
138. (c) Seoul in South Korea
139. An Enigma cipher machine
140. Ariel, *The Tempest*

P66

141. Codfish bones
142. *Two Years Before the Mast* by US author Richard Henry Dana, Jr.
143. USS *Abraham Lincoln*
144. (c) Reykjavik
145. Robert Newton, who portrayed Long John Silver on film
146. 'Farewell to Nova Scotia'
147. Eugene O'Neill
148. Don Sheppard
149. Robert Burns' 'Tam o' Shanter', named after the short chemise she wears
150. The Battle of Trafalgar

P67

151. (a) Five
152. (a) Hauled over a hill
153. HMS *Somerset*
154. (a) *Aurora*
155. Buster Keaton
156. Davy Crockett
157. The catamaran
158. *Demeter*
159. Stuart Woods
160. 'Spanish Ladies'

Science

P68

1. There may be two high waters and two low waters per day or just one of each
2. (c) Drogue
3. To measure the angle between two objects, most commonly a star or planet, such as the sun or the North Star, and the horizon
4. To direct air from outside to the inside of a ship
5. Usually true north, adjusted from a magnetic compass bearing
6. The angular distance of a location north or south of the equator. The North Pole is located at 90° north
7. The angular distance east or west of the Greenwich meridian, eg New York City has a longitude of 74°W
8. (a) London
9. To raise the head of the mainsail, and sometimes to tension the luff of the sail
10. (b) Magellanic Clouds

P69

11. (b) Nothing, the CQR originally was going to be called the 'secure' anchor
12. A chart of daily high and low waters at a particular location
13. Almost always wind action; changes in atmospheric pressure and seismic activity are also possible causes
14. Its scale is one sixth of a full rotation (60°)
15. When the boat is at right angles to the wind
16. A strut that runs across a boat from side to side forming a seat
17. (c) A short length of rope, sometimes with the ends joined
18. A lookout point
19. By flying NC (November Charlie)
20. An imaginary line cutting through all meridians at the same angle on a chart

P70

21. At the aft end of the foot of a sail
22. Inflated animal bladders or skins
23. (b) To reduce sail
24. It is where two oceans meet resulting in high winds, unpredictable waves and even icebergs
25. The speed at which the wavelength of the boat's bow wave (in displacement mode) is equal to the boat length
26. Nothing, it is just a distress signal (not 'Save Our Souls')
27. The first transatlantic telegraph cable
28. (c) Cork
29. An ornamental knot used to provide a stopper or thrower on the end of a line
30. A series of waves caused by the displacement of a large body of water, caused by volcanic or seismic activity, explosions, meteorite strikes etc

P71

31. The pointed part of an anchor that digs into the seabed
32. (a) Approximately 3.5 per cent
33. (b) Vertical stripes
34. An improvised form of ammunition in which chain links, nails, pebbles and other materials were fired from a cannon
35. The difference in wind speed and direction over a set distance
36. (b) The brain, confused by the contradictory data received from the eyes and the inner ear (balance)
37. (b) They have a double hull
38. The time when a tidal current ceases but hasn't yet turned; it usually occurs near high water and low water
39. Because salt water is heavier, it exerts a greater upward force on an object
40. An anchor ball forward by day, and a masthead light by night

P72

41. Cold water, as the molecules are closer together
42. A basin that can be flooded and drained to allow a vessel to rest on a platform for repairs or inspection
43. A penguin
44. The hovercraft
45. The Galapagos Islands
46. (c) Sydney
47. RMS *Titanic*
48. A spar projecting forward from the bow of a boat, enabling more sail to be carried
49. When the bow of the vessel is headed into wind and stalled, unable to manoeuvre
50. Either the third mast on a three-masted boat or the mast behind the main mast on a two-masted boat

P73

51. (a) Self-hire yacht chartering
52. Typically at the very bow of a sailing boat
53. When a sailing vessel turns its stern through the wind – very dangerous without proper control of the boom
54. At the stern
55. (a) Decoration of ivory or bone objects
56. (b) An opening bridge
57. To prevent leakage of water through carvel planks or clinker (lapstrake) boards
58. (b) Sailing a boat with the wind about 30° either side of dead downwind
59. (a) Griping
60. Channel 16 (156.8 MHz)

P74

61. Roll, pitch and yaw (also surge, sway and heave)
62. (a) Roach
63. Phosphorescence
64. A mass of small metal cannonballs packed into a cloth bag, which spread out upon firing

65. The parallels of latitude and meridians of longitude are shown as straight lines crossing each other at right angles
66. A wave is caused by wind action; a swell is what remains when the wind ceases to blow
67. A rule of thumb for estimating tidal height between low and high water
68. The Pole Star which points, within a degree or two, to true north
69. The branch of physics concerned with the behaviour of water, in relation to sailing
70. (c) Scrubbing wooden decks

P75

71. (a) A small light sail on a square rigged ship
72. A nautical mile is based on the circumference of the Earth, and is equal to one minute of latitude. A knot is one nautical mile per hour (1 knot = 1.85km/1.15 miles per hour)
73. (b) Greta Garbo
74. In a thunderstorm; it's a strong rotating updraft
75. (a) Growler
76. (c) Teach's lights
77. A short, smoothbore, cast-iron cannon, first produced by the Carron company in Scotland in the late 18th century
78. (c) The Vikings, to check bearings
79. Sailors in the northern hemisphere, to determine local time by reading the position of the stars
80. (b) The borders of channels

P76

81. (a) The British Royal Navy in the 18th century
82. A system for classifying hurricanes from category 1 (weakest) to 5 (strongest)
83. A nickname for the first inflatable lifejacket
84. Points of equal stational pressure at sea level (readings are reduced to sea level when an isobar crosses land)
85. (b) 20,200km (12,600 miles)
86. On the port, or left, side
87. An emergency position-indicating radio beacon used to aid the detection and location of boats in distress
88. A masthead light forward and a second masthead light abaft of and higher than this (vessels less than 50m (164ft) LOA are excused this); sidelights; a stern light
89. A tsunami arising from weather conditions such as a tropical cyclone
90. Seelonce Mayday

P77

91. The measurement and description of physical features associated with oceans, seas, lakes and rivers
92. You are inbound; buoy numbers increase as you approach land
93. (a) To the west

94. The front dips down suddenly into the water, causing it to decelerate quickly
95. To stabilise and act as a brake in heavy weather, rather than to tether to the seabed
96. (a) Globster
97. (b) The lowest level of a body of water
98. On the starboard side
99. (c) Less than 50m (164ft)
100. (c) At least four

P78

101. Bleeding gums, loose teeth, sore joints, bleeding under the skin, anaemia, slow wound healing, fatigue
102. (b) 71 per cent
103. Sidelights and a stern light (this also applies to a vessel under oars)
104. Mainly along the longitude of 180°, with adjustments to avoid islands in the north and south
105. A strong current, specifically one that rips past the southern end of the Lofoten Islands off the coast of Norway
106. (a) Between 8 and 12
107. (b) Preventer
108. Mayday
109. The mainsail configuration used on most yachts, with a triangular sail aft of the mast whose head is attached to the top of the mast and whose clew is attached to the end of a boom
110. To tension the aft edge (the leech) of a sail if it is fluttering once set

P79

111. To tension the roach, the additional material added to the triangle of sail formed between the clew, the tack and the head
112. (c) Scow
113. The distance from the waterline to the lowest point on deck at which water can enter a boat
114. To tighten the clew of the sail along the boom
115. The amount of overlap with the mainsail; a jib will not overlap by more than about 20 per cent, while a genoa may overlap the mainsail entirely
116. (a) Bernoulli's principle
117. (b) St Elmo's fire
118. Between 156.0 and 162.025 MHz inclusive
119. Checking to see if a light disappears over the horizon if the observer's eye height is quickly dropped (if it does, the navigation light is at its geographical range)
120. The lateral (side-to-side) curvature of a boat deck. Curvature adds strength and allows water to run off

P80

121. (a) A legal term for the intentional damage of a vessel or its cargo
122. (b) 1810
123. (a) The hydrological cycle
124. Naval gunfire directed parallel to the long axis of an enemy ship
125. (a) 1875
126. The point immediately above

the observer's position on Earth, so a straight line passes through the centre of the earth, and the position of the observer, to the zenith

127. Two anchors set 45° apart or at wider angles up to 90°

128. (b) A standing wave oscillating in a body of water

129. (c) *Nereus* reached 11km (6.8 miles) in 2009

130. The European Union and the European Space Agency

P81

131. The action of naming all 32 points of the compass, in order clockwise

132. (c) A ship's latitude

133. (a) Isaac Newton (who invented a reflecting quadrant in about 1699, although he never published his work)

134. The name given to the wind when it blows onto the beam of a vessel under sail

135. (b) Two

136. (a) The Bristol Channel, between England and Wales

137. (a) GLONASS (Global Navigation Satellite System)

138. (b) The Greek historian Thucydides in 426 BCE

139. Testing the hull designs of ships

140. (c) An angel

P82

141. (a) A hydrographic survey in South America

142. (a) 40cm (16in)

143. (b) Bruce anchor

144. The shortest route across the sea between any two points, known as the orthodromic distance

145. The stockless anchor

146. (a) 1978

147. The depth of the sea. It is the aquatic equivalent of a topographic relief map

148. When starting off, the craft must ride over the bow wave that forms in front of it

149. (b) Ox-eye

150. To keep time at sea accurately. By comparing the time at their home port with ship time, navigators could work out their longitude

P83

151. One long blast followed by three short blasts, repeated at two-minute intervals

152. (b) 10–20cm (4–8in)

153. A triangular sail with spars along its upper and lower edges, much used in the Pacific Ocean

154. The Vikings

155. (a) Sheer

156. The halo is caused by a refraction through ice crystals, often a sign of wet weather approaching

157. (b) An alidade

158. (a) A combined smokestack and mast

159. The wind experienced on a moving boat is made up of true wind

and the wind you feel because of movement, which is apparent wind

160. (b) Trilateration (triangulation involves measuring angles as well)

Trivia

P84

1. (b) Two
2. Sea
3. To tie a bowline knot
4. (b) Move ahead
5. Plimsoll Line (mark)
6. (a) Ship is about to sail and all persons should report on board
7. (b) 'Haul yards' – haul up the spar on the big sails
8. (a) Fastnet Race
9. (a) A spar fixed on board a ship used for hoisting cargo
10. (a) *Star of India*

P85

11. Midnight on New Year's Eve
12. The sinking of RMS *Titanic*
13. U-boat
14. Germany
15. On sick leave
16. Weight of the crew
17. Convention on the International Regulations for Preventing Collisions at Sea, 1972
18. Royal Mail Ship – contracted by the British postal company to carry mail
19. (b) Mid-18th century
20. Johnny Depp

P86

21. Length of a ship's anchor cable
22. (c) Ten
23. (c) Phoenix Islands
24. Junk
25. Because it's a flogging over the cannon
26. (a) One mast, one sail
27. (a) USS *Constitution*
28. (a) To smarten or tidy up
29. (a) A commander
30. *The Golden Hind*

P87

31. (b) Two
32. Atlas
33. *The Love Boat*
34. International Maritime Organization
35. (a) Whaling
36. Ditch, drink
37. At the stern
38. The bireme
39. (a) It was cut off and suspended from the bow of First Lieutenant Maynard's sloop
40. (b) 'Stop, and listen to me'

P88

41. (a) An unofficial award for the fastest crossing of the Atlantic Ocean
42. (a) Zephyrus
43. (b) To disguise their outline
44. Royal Marines
45. (a) Christ child

46. Beaching it for cleaning or repair
47. No, it's another name for a cat-o'-nine tails
48. ((b) Arguing
49. (c) 28,000
50. Three times (Mayday, Mayday, Mayday)

P89

51. Keel
52. The cat o'nine tails from the red baize bag
53. Animal
54. Drink it; it is slang for rum
55. (a) Foreign currency
56. Venice: Laguna Veneta; laguna meaning 'pool' or 'lake'
57. (c) Dartmouth, UK
58. (c) Belfast, Northern Ireland
59. *Mary Celeste*
60. (c) 66

P90

61. Store rooms, junior officers' cabins, medical bay, engine room
62. Bono
63. (a) Dirty or untidy
64. Bing Crosby
65. *Jolie Brise*
66. SS *Californian*
67. *Australia II* beat *Liberty*
68. HMY *Britannia*
69. The first ship from which Radio Caroline was broadcast
70. Planks overlap in clinker planking; planks are fastened edge-to-edge in carvel planking

P91

71. The 'painted' or 'spotted' one
72. 'Calypso'
73. (a) Pigs' bladders
74. Top of the mast ie the highest sail
75. (a) RMS *Mauretania*
76. (a) Foreign Object Damage
77. Stewed prunes
78. Greenwich, London, UK
79. (c) Full-time Navy
80. (c) Retiring from sea life and settling down ashore

P92

81. (b) Bamboozle
82. RMS *Queen Mary*, travelling at 28 knots
83. Errol Flynn
84. (b) A sailor's name for shoes worn by Royal Marines for shore service
85. A picnic party
86. (c) 1,198
87. The Pharos of Alexandria
88. (a) USA – 19 gold, 23 silver, 17 bronze
89. (b) Marconi rig
90. (a) Sandbagger

P93

91. Dennis Wilson of the *Beach Boys*
92. Tony Bullimore
93. (c) A female character similar to a mermaid in Aboriginal mythology
94. (b) Rupert Brooke
95. (c) Scotland
96. No, they are food or drink stains
97. A sailor's name for heavy boots

worn by Royal Marines
98. Tropical Fresh water
99. (c) In a weak position
100. (b) 1851

P94

101. Any one of Dover, Sandwich, Hastings, Romney or Hythe
102. Switzerland
103. (a) Zulu time
104. (b) In the Nao Victoria Museum, Punta Arenas, Chile
105. SS *United States*
106. Balsa logs lashed together with hemp ropes. No metal was used to build the raft
107. (c) Blue
108. 'Port outward, starboard home' referred to the best accommodation on a ship travelling out to India and back to Britain (ie not in full sunlight)
109. Donald Crowhurst
110. Proud; it is gold braid embroidered on senior officers' caps

P95

111. (c) 1,503
112. (a) Auld Mug
113. (c) Useless bits of material
114. (a) Whitby collier
115. Martin Luther King, Jnr
116. Sir Francis Drake
117. Robert Maxwell
118. The liaison between King Edward VIII and Wallis Simpson
119. (a) 53
120. *Jolie Brise*

P96

121. The America's Cup
122. Athene, carved out of talking oak
123. (b) Two fathoms (3.7m/12ft)
124. *Santana*, owned by Humphrey Bogart
125. China
126. (c) The Baltic Sea
127. BOC Challenge
128. Natalie Wood
129. *Atlantic Crossing*
130. The ship was sunk in the Atlantic ocean after being torpedoed by a German U-boat

P97

131. (a) Robert Foulis
132. (a) The Uluburun
133. (b) Rosehearty
134. (a) 1952
135. James Dyson
136. (b) As a coastguard ship on the Essex coast in the UK, before being sold for breaking up in 1870
137. Richard Burton for Elizabeth Taylor
138. (c) An incompetent officer
139. (c) The Rhine
140. Neva Yacht Club in St Petersburg

P98

141. Oracle Team
142. (a) *Atlantic Daily Bulletin*
143. (b) 1900, in Paris. Scheduled for Greece in 1896, but races were cancelled due to bad weather
144. Sir Arthur Conan Doyle

145. (c) *Venus*
146. New York, 123 immigrants
147. (a) 1982
148. Queen Elizabeth I
149. SS *United States*
150. Tycho Brahe

P99

151. (a) Salvation, hope and religious steadfastness
152. *Taeping*, which sailed from Fuzhou to Gravesend in 102 days
153. Venez m'aider (come and help me)
154. GK Chesterton
155. (b) The Clermont
156. The Tri Lake Challenge
157. *Athena*, *Maltese Falcon* or *Mirabella V*
158. The tsunami wave from the Lisbon earthquake
159. (b) Saddam Hussein
160. The US Gulf Coast; Lake Pontchartrain in Louisiana to Gulfport, Mississippi

Quick-fire

P100

1. Starboard
2. Port
3. Bow
4. Stern
5. Head
6. Galley
7. Hull
8. Helm
9. Six
10. Fender

P101

11. Squall
12. Tiller
13. Ground tackle
14. Astern
15. Gangway
16. Stow
17. Heading
18. Draft
19. Beam
20. Mutiny

P102

21. Wash
22. Avast
23. Pontoon
24. Becalmed
25. Lee shore
26. Clove hitch
27. Jonah
28. Knot
29. Furl
30. Bight

P103

31. Gunwales
32. Stowaway
33. Pennant
34. Cleat
35. Nautical mile
36. Rowlock
37. Luff
38. Sheet
39. Binnacle
40. Ready about

Acknowledgements

The publisher would like to thank Shutterstock
for their kind permission to reproduce the images in this book.

We have made every effort to ensure that the answers provided in this book are factually accurate but please let us know if you spot any that you think are incorrect.